A Brief Instruction in Christian Religion

Questions and Answers (with new material)

By

Faustus Socinus

of Siena

Circa 1590

Translation by: William Fontana Sr., M.A.

fontana-art

fontana-art.com

1

ISBN-13: 978-1492989592

ISBN-10: 1492989592

William Fontana Sr, M.A.

Cover designed by William Fontana Jr.

ACKNOWLEDGEMENT

This book would not have been possible to write without a great deal of help and support. First, without the intellectual strength, faith and courage of my lovely wife Marsha, it is hard to imagine that I would have had the stability, or necessary strength to complete this work. My children, grandchildren, and all children everywhere have inspired me to hope for a continuation of a world heritage of intellectual and physical freedom, and because of my love of children, I am stronger in the realization of how important it is for us to work for the preservation of their future natural environment, especially, of wonderful wild places.

I have been blessed with wonderful teachers. My college professors have given me the tools of the intellect! Of special import to me was my brilliant friend and Latin professor, the late Dr. Günter Mecke.

As a tour guide in Yosemite, I have enjoyed the company of and learned from my fellow tour guides, Karen Blakely, Frank Bonaventura, Alan Bragg, Carol Bragg, Julie Chavez, Michael Dyer, Bill Fagan, Sam Hays, Emily Jacobs, Charles Lammers,

Dave O'Brien, Herb Parsons, Jack Peters, Jim Simpkins, Chuck Whitney and others. The thousands of guests who have been on my tours have inspired me with their love of Yosemite. They have also supported and helped educate me with their questions and comments. I have many special friends in Yosemite who have greatly enriched my life simply by being good friends!

My friend, Crystal Grippen, shares my love of the Latin language, and she has been of great help to me (she restored a copy of the original Latin script that I had lost). Herb Parsons has taken the time to proofread my manuscript and made many necessary corrections. He has also suggested improvements to help the reader understand the polemic form. Joseph Michael Gormley Connors has taken the time to read the manuscript and his insights on the problems of the Socinian lexicon have resulted in a small glossary and a notation in the introduction as to the problem of understanding the revolutionary Christian language of Socinus. Joseph also pointed out many errors in the text, which I have corrected. Also, Barbara Minor has done an excellent job of reading, in order to make grammatical and spelling corrections, as well as corrections in significant research errors. Barbara has been the force behind this corrected version. The Yosemite Valley Research librarian Linda Eade, has helped me with necessary rare research materials, and her help has been essential.

Without the national park we call Yosemite and the Park Service who protect it, I would not have had the refuge, strength, or education to finish this work. I have been educated and inspired, like millions of others, by the life and work of John Muir.

Finally, my greatest acknowledgement, and gratitude has to be for the life and teachings of the master himself, Jesus Christ.

FORWARD

My intent in writing this book is to share with the reader a part of
my journey to better understand the religious and intellectual
history of the western world. Through this work, I do *not* seek to
alter religious or political opinions.

My translation of Fausto Sozzini's (<u>Christianae Religionis
Brevissima Institutio</u> 1656) in 1980 was nearly a *verbatim*
translation.   In this revised edition, I have done my best to
include the passion and drama that certainly were intended to be
a part of the theological duel that was destined to change the

history of the world. After practicing the art of interpretation for many years (as a Yosemite tour guide), I have applied the *art of interpretation* to this *translation* in order to bring alive Sozzini's portrayal of two intrepid theologians and to give this work life in contemporary American English, and to allow Sozzini (through a *small* portion his life's work), to speak to the English reader directly.

In the 16th and 17th centuries, the method of choice for theologians to present their opinions was called a *polemic*. <u>A Very Brief Instruction in Christian Religion</u> is an example of a (*polemic*). The polemic form, used in the sixteenth century to argue religious opinion, was modeled after the Greek classical dialogue. In the high form of the polemic, the author would include both sides of a given argument. The idea was to be confident enough of one's opinion to fairly present other opinions usually through a question-and-answer format. One could say that with the intellectual-philosophical writing of the 18th (through 21st centuries,) we see a greater and greater reliance on propaganda. In the light of our present time, you may find Sozzini's polemic form very different and hopefully, somewhat refreshing.

Fausto Sozzini was and is very revolutionary in his theological opinions. He was so revolutionary for his time period that one could have been imprisoned, burned at the stake, or both, in the sixteenth, seventeenth and eighteenth centuries throughout most of Europe, for possessing or holding what are called Socinian opinions; i.e., he was not called the arch heretic without reason. After over four centuries, many of the readers of this translation will find the Socinian lexicon very different from a traditional understanding of terms and words in Christianity, and that is to be expected. *One should be aware that as an incomplete list:*

sanctification, gospel, world, human nature, time, new creatures, atonement, holy spirit, primary ascension, sacrifice, intercession, justification, redemption, priesthood, the nature of god, and salvation, all have been explained in a unique way by Sozzini. I have included a glossary of single words and terms, and in addition, Sozzini to a certain extent through his polemic explains the contrasting definitions of some theological terms not included in the glossary.

Finally, the name Faustus Socinus is a Latinized form of Fausto Sozzini. Both names are used in the text; I use Faustus Socinus in the more formal cases, like the title, but when I am referring to him in other areas, I use his Italian given name. Also, in the original Latin version, the dialogue has a prefatory "interrog or respon". I have deleted these in the translation as it is easy to follow this back-and-forth dialogue between two theologians who are very different in their style of presentation, and theological opinions.

BIOGRAPHICAL INFORMATION ABOUT FAUSTO SOZZINI

Fausto Sozzini the Italian religious reformer, was born in Siena, Italy on December 5, 1539.   He was the only son of Alessandro Sozzini and Agnese Borghese Petrucci. By giving up the life of wealth and splendor of the Tuscan court to pursue his religious ideals, "Sozzini condemned himself to run through the nations as an unfortunate vagabond." Fausto was married in 1586 to Elizabeth Morsztyn in Pawlikowice, Poland. In 1587 Fausto and Elizabeth had one daughter, Agnese. In September of that same year, Fausto's wife Elizabeth died.   Fausto died on March 3, 1604, at Luslawice, Poland. [1] The following inscription was made on his monument at Luslawice.

Total licet Babylon destruxit tecta Lutherus Calvinus muros sed Fundamenta Socinus [2]

(The whole of the licentiousness of Babylon was not destroyed by the roof of Luther or by the walls of Calvin, but by the foundation of Sozzini.)

A JOURNEY TO BETTER UNDERSTAND THE
THEOLOGICAL-PHILOSOPHICAL WORK OF FAUSTO SOZZINI

The year was 1977, and I was working as a post graduate student at California State University Hayward, (now the University of the East Bay). I had completed my Bachelor's Degree in Art with honors, and was working on a post graduate course of study in foreign languages (Latin, Spanish, French, Italian, German, and a little Greek). Along with my study of foreign languages, I was studying fine art printmaking.

In retrospect, I cannot imagine a more wonderful or brilliant group of professors than the ones I would study under at Cal State Hayward, while embarking upon my linguistic, philosophical, and artistic adventure. There were Dr. Correa Zoli (Italian and Italian ethnicity), Dr. Thomas Watson (French), Rudolpho Galan (Spanish), and Dr. Gunter Mecke (Latin). And I must also mention my art and printmaking Master, Kenji Nanao. *These professors inspired, as well as educated.*

As I studied foreign languages, I was also reading English translations of the great names in philosophy. I was reading about one book a week (Schopenhauer, Hegel, Hume, Kant, Freud, Einstein, Adam Smith, Karl Marx, Carl Jung, Plato, Voltaire, Nietzsche, Rousseau, and others. We can stop at Rousseau because it was with Jean Jacques that my reading pace was to be broken and my story of this translation begins.

I read in an article, "Voltaire and the Socinians,"[3] that both Rousseau and Voltaire had been accused of being Socinians. I simply put the name Faustus Socinus (Latinized version of Fausto Sozzini) on my reading list, and read on. It was sometime later, when I was in the California State Hayward library (where I worked as a student librarian), having failed to find any material translated from the work of the controversial Faustus Socinus, I inquired of a senior librarian; "Do we have anything written by Faustus Socinus, or translated from his <u>own</u> work?" Together we searched and found only a few materials that made reference to Sozzini: one short biography: <u>Faustus Socinus</u>, by David Cory; a book written in Italian about Italian heretics: <u>Gle Ertetici D'Italia Disorsi Storici,</u> by Cesare Cantu`; and a book on Socinianism in Poland: <u>Socinianism in Poland</u>, by Stanislas Kot.

Short of having something written by Sozzini, or translated from his own work, I studied the materials that we found. I learned that Socinians were persecuted in Poland, and their books burned in Europe. The Socinian religious heresy was viewed as an anathema throughout Europe in the sixteenth and seventeenth centuries.[4] *I read that the Socinians refused to fight in wars, rejected capital punishment, denied the holy Trinity, they taught that Jesus was human in nature, and they based salvation on reason alone.[5]*

My research also indicated that the theological work of Fausto Sozzini was credited with playing a major role in the development of the Age of Enlightenment, humanism, new science, tolerance of varied religious opinion, and <u>Unitarianism</u>![6] He was credited with influencing the work of many philosophers: Locke, Hume, Rousseau, and others.[7] Of course this would mean that politically Socinianism was fundamental to the American Revolution and

Constitution of the United States. Not having any written material or translations of Sozzini's work, I was not satisfied! I became curious.

I wondered how could a historical figure of the intellectual and religious importance of Fausto Sozzini, not be translated into English? Was there residual fear, disdain, and suppression of his work from the sixteenth and seventeenth centuries, and if that was the case, how could that be? Or was there some historical reason his theological work was *not* available in English?

It was at this juncture that I started to *speculate*. My speculation would lead me down a path that would greatly increase my respect for the *intellectual freedom* we enjoy in the United States, and my respect for the *Christian religion* as well. The speculation also began my *quest!*

The thought occurred to me: *"At the heart of the spirit of the Constitution of the United States, is freedom of speech and religion."* It occurred to me that if any of Sozzini's work had survived the *book burning* in Europe and Russia in the sixteenth, seventeenth, eighteenth, and twentieth centuries, there might be a book containing his work in the large library at the University of California at Berkeley. I was without a car at that time, so I took the BART transportation system to Berkeley. I entered the large university library, and was awestruck by the size of the collection. Having worked as a student librarian in the university library at Hayward, I knew that I was looking for the rare book collection.

I was directed to an upstairs room. It was upon entering the rare book collection area at the University of California at Berkeley that I learned the meaning of "tome" as compared to book. I asked the librarian: "Do you have anything written by Fausto Sozzini? He answered, "Yes".

Have you ever had an experience in your life where you would have been willing to bet (ten to one) your plans would not work out as you hoped, or what you were trying to do would not get done? This was such an experience. I really believed that this trip to the university library at Berkeley was futile, or a long shot at best. I was really surprised when the librarian returned with an ancient tome (about 380 years old) in his hands.

It is hard to describe the wonder and emotions of looking down at my hands while they held this nearly four-hundred-year-old book!

<u>(The **OPERA OMNIA** (Complete Works) Vol. I by Faustus Socinus, dated 1656)</u>

My first thoughts were: *I am relieved and grateful that this book had survived!* Then *I think, the book sure looks good for being nearly 400 years old! And, finally (among some) there must have been a great deal of respect for Sozzini's work to publish these volumes in the seventeenth century (52 years after Sozzini's death).* I reverently took my treasure to a table, sat down, and <u>very</u> carefully started turning the pages. The book was written in Latin.

After studying the tome for awhile, I was able to determine that there was a small (but very important) portion of this book, which given enough time I could translate:

<u>A Brief Instruction in Christian Religion</u>

I also thought it's likely this small part of Sozzini's complete works would answer my questions about Socinian thought, theology, and give me a chance to understand Socinianism from the *source*. I explained my interest in Sozzini to the librarian, and then I asked: *"Can I copy A Brief Instruction in Christian Religion?"* Then *I got my second great surprise of the day. The librarian answered, "Yes!"*

The librarian treated my requests with great respect and even helped copy Sozzini's: Very Brief Instruction in Christian Religion.

I went home with my Latin treasure, feeling like Dr. Howard Carter when he discovered King Tut's tomb.

What followed was a period of great intellectual diversity in my life. I was continuing my linguistic studies, working on my figure drawings and prints (preparing for a show of my figure drawings at Chabot College in 1978), and with my Latin and Greek dictionaries, Bible, and textbooks, laboriously translating the Brief Instruction in Christian Religion, line for line. I looked up all of the scriptural references and checked them. *It was amazing to see that these nearly four hundred year old scriptural citations in the Latin work matched perfectly with my (King James) version of the Bible.*

Now my hurried race to understand the history of the western world's evolution in religion, philosophy and genius had completely stalled, and I was being changed in the process, as I tried to figure out what the man (who seemed to be in the shadows of sixteenth century western world history) had to say for himself. It seemed that a major piece of a historical puzzle was missing! I spent over 1000 hours translating the Latin word for word, sentence for sentence. *In reality, what I lacked in genius, I made up for in dogged determination!*

In the end, I finished the translation, and after my wife Marsha reworked the very awkward English sentences (produced from a very *verbatim translation)*, we copyrighted the translation in **1980**. The English version was a nearly *verbatim* translation of the original Latin that comprised **129** pages in English. Through this work, I had gained a much better understanding of the brilliance, thought, and theology of Fausto Sozzini. *Now I understood that some of what I had read (at that time) about Sozzini was distorted and incorrect (highly akin to political sound bites), and the rest was so erudite as to be written mostly for theologians.* I was exhausted from the work. I copied my work for a few friends.

My course of study in college would return solely to making images. I was accepted in the masters program at California State University in Chico, and moved to Chico with my wife Marsha.

At the completion of my master's program at CSUC in art (Drawing and Painting), a member of the faculty said to me, "It is time for you to go to New York and make a name for yourself with your art". I must say this thought came as a shock to me, as I never intended to wind up in a big city. *I have always loved wilderness and rural life, and I had come to Chico in 1981 partly to escape the city life of the San Francisco Bay Area.*

As a little boy, I grew up in Castro Valley in the East San Francisco Bay Area. In the 1950's, Castro Valley was a magical place for a little boy. My brother Joe and I lived in a foster home where we had horses, chickens, dogs, snakes, and many other pets. *I did not learn as much in grade school as I should have because I was too busy following my wild instincts. Supervision of my activities was minimal, thank goodness!* My ability to freely roam the wild hills of Castro Valley as a child had instilled in me a love of the wild. A group of us little boys formed the Boy's Wild Life Club. I was the president!

My love of the wild (and rural geography) was part of the reason that after my pursuit of a Master's Degree in Art at California State University Chico was successful in 1984, I came to Yosemite National Park to make images. I guess that I knew fame and fortune were not waiting for me as a Yosemite painter. Like so many other artists, I wanted to come to Yosemite to strengthen my spirit and to produce images inspired by Yosemite's beauty. I was drawn to Yosemite's wilderness and beauty, like a moth to a light bulb.

I did not know it at the time, but in a way, when I arrived in Yosemite, I was being drawn back to my translation. An artist (of little notoriety), must support themselves by working at a regular job. As they say: "Don't give up your day job." I had a history of working in transportation (truck driving, dock work, and bus driving) throughout much of my life, so I was a natural to drive a bus!

After spending the summer of 1983 as the Yosemite Valley ice man, I returned in 1985 to work driving a Yosemite Valley shuttle bus. Working for the Yosemite Transportation System, I learned that there was the possibility of giving tours in Yosemite as a driver guide. I wanted to advance so I could become a driver-guide; therefore, when I returned to Chico, I studied the history of Yosemite in the California State University Library at Chico.

I studied the lives and work of the great people who were responsible for the beginnings of the Yosemite Land Grant (1864), and Yosemite National Park (1890) in the nineteenth century. I came to realized that people such as Abraham Lincoln, Galen Clark, Israel Raymond, John Muir, and Theodore Roosevelt (to name a few) were veritable giants for their courage, brilliance and dedication to the conservation of public land for our future well-being. *I also discovered that the "idea for national parks" began in Yosemite.*

Studying, working hard, having a positive attitude, and above all, being very grateful for my opportunity to live and work in Yosemite, all helped me to become a better tour guide. *And, all the hours of research, followed by thousands of hours of verbal presentation (while driving a bus), have greatly increased my ability to organize my thoughts in a clear and concise manner for the purpose of interpretation.*

I have had the privilege of giving about 1000 (Yosemite National Park) Grand Tours. The Grand Tour dates from the nineteenth century, and it exists today as a Yosemite all day bus tour of Glacier Point, the Wawona Hotel, and the Mariposa Grove of Giant Sequoias. Today the Grand Tour is geographically the same tour that has been given by the Yosemite conservation giants, Galen Clark and John Muir (and, of course, many others). Often on the Grand Tour, I would have about 40 people who had come to Yosemite from various parts of the United States and the world. *One day I was privileged to have two senators: one from South Carolina, and one from South Korea!*

As a Yosemite tour guide, I have always done my best to use the best research and provide people with an honest and straightforward interpretation of the wonders of *Yosemite. For example, I would not hesitate to point out that the California air pollution problem (that can be seen so well by observing the inversion layer in the San Joaquin Valley, looking out from*

Highway 41 from between the Wawona Tunnel and the Glacier Point intersection), and talk about the devastation that air pollution is having in the forests of Yosemite and world forests (through acid rain and global warming). When interpreting the history of Yosemite, I would say this: "There are three things that a wise tour guide should <u>not</u> discuss on a tour: one is politics, two is religion (a subject that humans often kill one another over), and three is love (romance)". Of course, I would then go on to say, "I will be careful to talk about all three" (usually a laugh at this point). Then I would qualify: "Am I looking forward to a new line of work by taking this approach? Am I tired of giving tours and really want a way out? I would then answer my rhetorical questions by saying, "No, I really like my job, but for the life of me, I find it very difficult to explain Yosemite's amazing history, or any history for that matter, if those aspects of human history were ignored! After all, they are primary human motivators!"

I am very grateful to say that in all the years (of my plainly spoken style of touring), I know of no complaints from my guests because I talked about the religious and political roots of the birth of the idea of national parks. I really wanted to do my best, to speak honestly, from accurate research, and live up to the trust that had been placed in me, i.e. to walk boldly in the shoes of the conservation giants like John Muir.

That having been said, it would be remiss of me (forgetful of my own research into the life of Fausto Sozzini and the roots of Unitarianism) not to notice the disproportionate number of Unitarians, among the early nature writers in the United States who were in love with American wilderness and champions of public land conservation.

Among these early pioneers of public land conservation were, deists, romantics, transcendentalists, spiritualists, Unitarians, freethinkers, or you could just call them nature lovers. *When you study their lives and thought, you soon realize they were not exceptionally traditional in their religious beliefs. Also, I know of none that did not believe in God, or were irreligious!* Their departure from traditional Christian religious opinion was centered in their love of pure wilderness. *They found divinity in wilderness, and believed man's God-given "dominion" and commandment to "subdue the wilderness" needed to be modified.* As representative of the passion that these pioneers of conservation of wilderness felt John Muir stated, *"From the Wilderness take only your memories, leave only your footprints."*

It did not come easy for European pioneers entering the American wilderness to behold the wilderness and say, *"The best thing that we can do with this particular untamed and commercially valuable wild place (considering our God given right of dominion and license to subdue the Earth "Genesis I: 24-28"), is to keep our mitts off!"* *This tremendous change in religious and political opinion toward nature and public land policy required a religious and philosophical revolution, i.e. a new viewpoint and interpretation of "biblical dominion" that would establish the importance of stewardship, i.e., less greed and arrogance, and a greater understanding of our human limitations and human need for purely wild places. Further, for this revolution to be successful, it had to be embraced by those of traditional religious and cultural opinions.*

It is in the political and religious revolution that took place in the nineteenth century (that would lead to creation of National Parks), we find the distinctive historical Unitarian marks of Fausto Sozzini.

The following is a brief summary of the 19th century American debt to the Unitarian religious tradition that spawned the most potent force in the birth of National Parks which was the art and poetry of transcendental idealism. Ralph Waldo Emerson the author of <u>Nature</u> (1836) and the father of American Transcendentalism, was a Unitarian preacher's son, and was ordained as a Unitarian minister in 1829.[8] Henry David Thoreau was Emerson's student and devoted to Emerson's Transcendentalism. Galen Clark (who drew the first physical transcendental boundary around the Mariposa grove of giant sequoias and who was the first guardian of the Yosemite land grant) was raised as a Unitarian and had two brothers who were Unitarian pastors. In later life Galen Clark became a Spiritualist).[9] & [15] John Muir parted from the theology of his father Daniel a Calvinistic preacher, and moved toward Emerson's Transcendentalism.[10] John Muir was without a doubt the most successful in establishing transcendental idealism as the preservation-conservation model for national parks. Also noteworthy were the early public land preservation-conservation efforts made through the writing and poetry of Reverend Star King, the nineteenth century Unitarian preacher.[11] & [16] *After taking note of the influence of Unitarian tradition in the lives of those whose poetry, writing, and decisions played such a major role in the birth of national parks one can without a doubt connect the deep theological roots of transcendentalism to the Unitarian tradition of theological dissent and Socinianism.*

As I have done hundreds of times, one day I was standing at the Wawona Tunnel view in Yosemite National Park looking out at the world famous view of Yosemite Valley and Half Dome. This view looks very much like it has for thousands of years, i.e., no building, roads, or anything of human construction visible. It occurred to me, has the privilege of enjoying this spectacular unchanged view of the wilderness in the twenty-first century, come without a price?

It was at this juncture, that I saw the Socinian anti-Trinitarian heresy, and the persecution of Sozzini's followers as part of the price for the historical evolution in Christian religious opinion and attitude, that led to transcendentalism, and other forms of landscape idealism, and the beginning of preservation conservation.

And now it is time for the English reader to experience a theological duel that would send shockwaves through the centuries since it took place. Come with me and witness these two profound theologians fight a duel over the essential matters of Christian opinion and attitude. Please witness this duel, as a chance to appreciate the value of theologians and theological debate as an influence on philosophy and history. Perhaps like me, you will travel back in time; to visit two brave sixteenth century Polish theologians who dared to try to understand God and really cared about how correct Christian belief and opinion would influence the future of humanity!

A Brief Instruction in Christian Religion

by

Faustus Socinus

TABLE OF CONTENTS

CHRISTIAN RELIGION

What is Christian religion?

Christian religion is the divine path to immortality.

Are not humans innately immortal?

No

Why?

Humans were formed from the earth (Gen. 9:5), and created from that which is mortal (I Cor. 15:47). Also, they violated those teachings given to them by God (Gen.2:17, & 3:17 etc.) which resulted in the punishment of death.

So how do we follow the divine path?

We walk the path of enlightenment with Jesus in order to be united with God (John 17:3).

So what is enlightenment?

Primarily, it is that we unite our actions to the will of God according to the teachings of Jesus.

To do this do we need to understand the nature of Christ?

Yes, because this understanding helps us bring our ways into unity with the will of God.

GOD

Can't we understand the nature of God by understanding the nature of Christ?

No! We must address the nature of God and Christ separately.

Why is that?

I will explain later.

This seems strange; I am hopeful that you will explain yourself!

I will.

Then what is most important for us to believe about God, apart from Jesus?

First that he <u>is</u>, and secondly, that God is only <u>one</u> in number.

What do you mean when you say he is?

I mean that he is the source of the divine power within us.

What do you mean when you say that he is "only one"?

We must understand by his teachings that he <u>alone</u> is the source of the divine power within us.

What is this divine power within us?

It is the right, and also the power for us to accomplish the things which need to be done. Or to put this in another way, to accomplish the things that we could not do without the help of

God. *So let's not suffer from the delusion that the great things we accomplish (whether they are insights or deeds) are done by us alone, but rather they are accomplished by the divine power of God that ebbs and flows within our hearts.* And thus it is that the laws were imposed, and their rewards and punishments made.

Tell me more about this divine power.

It is the divine power which cannot be ascribed to any other source than God.

This all seems a bit confusing and obscure; can you do a better job explaining these ideas?

It is not easy to explain what is unique to divine power. *We can say that it only comes from God. We can also say that nothing can escape this power. We can also say that divine power belongs to God and therefore, cannot be transferred from one person to another. So the Scripture says, "God alone is potentate," (I Timothy 6:15).*

Could you please explain the wording of I Timothy 6:15?

Sure. Whatever is of human power is not the limit of divinity, and, yet divine power within humanity is a gift from God.

How does this relate to *time?*

We should believe that God is the author of eternity, and only through God can we come to eternal life. Thus it is that we are provided a path to eternal life through Jesus Christ.

Isn't there more to the nature of God?

Yes!

What else?

Within the nature of God are *justice, wisdom and infinite power.*

How do you define *divine justice?*

Essentially it is *honesty and equality.*

How do you define wisdom?

Wisdom is a profound knowledge and understanding of things.

And finally power?

Divine power is the faculty to do the will of God.

Is it essential for us to ascribe ultimate justice, wisdom and infinite power to God; in order to obey his will as shown to us by Jesus Christ?

Yes, it is.

Please tell more about these beliefs concerning the *nature of God.*

Let me first talk about justice *(honesty and equality).*

It is necessary for us to believe that God is the ultimate and perfect source of justice, i.e., honesty and equality. Also, if we desire to obey Jesus then we need to admit that God allows indignity because without freedom, the promises that God has made to us through Christ would mean nothing. For even though we all sin, we should not say that our own shortcomings have their roots in God, but rather that wrong comes from within us.

And now what do you say about *wisdom?*

As was the case with justice, we must believe that God has the perfect wisdom and knowledge of things. When we believe in our hearts that nothing is impossible to know through the highest perpetual wisdom and knowledge of God, we can find this wisdom and knowledge within ourselves. So it follows that no part of the understanding of wisdom is too difficult for humans.

And finally of *divine power*

It is always present. If we believe God can grant us eternal life, then we must believe in his omnipotence and power. Unless we believe everything to be in the hands of God, how else can we be free from evil through Jesus Christ? In other words it is only through God's plan that eternal promises are made and kept!

Well, you have made it clear that we should believe God is only one, *so what is singular to the nature of God?* And further, *are there other personages of God*, and if there are of what sort are they?

This question implies a *contradiction.*

How so?

In the sense that God is believed to be one, and yet, you raise ideas that imply there may be more to the faith in one God than meets the eye.

What do you mean?

You say he is believed to be one, and yet you ask if there are not more personages.

I must admit, concerning this point, I am a bit frustrated. There is the essence of God's nature on the one hand, and the question of his personages on the other. *So let me go over this one more time so there can be no doubt about what I am asking.* We believe that God is in <u>one,</u> in essence, and yet, with Jesus and the Holy Spirit, there are more personages that share what is essential to God. Now, do you have a problem with these traditional Christian beliefs?

Yes! Here is where the confusion lies. When you talk about the essence of God, you do not make the distinction in the first case of what is *specie essence,* and in the second, of *essence in connection with God's substance.* This distinction is important, for the specie essence of God is <u>one</u> in number, as is the essence of the person of God. Or to make this even clearer, *the only commonality than can be held with God is through the intellect,* of which we are endowed from God's specie essence, and certainly not with God's essence of person. *This is modeled in our human condition, in the way we share intellectual understanding, but not personages.*

I can see that your logic may have some value. Do you have more to add?

Yes. In (Deut 6:4 etc,) it clearly states, as our discussion has brought out that *God is only one in number.* Or could we not say that if God has more than *one divine person,* then there would be possibly *many divine essences?*

Is it *essential* that we agree with these beliefs in order to attain eternal life?

We certainly should always ascribe to the truth, but to say this was a primary condition to attain salvation would be wrong!

Again you surprise me. According to common Christian belief, a correct understanding of faith is essential for salvation, so what are you saying?

I am saying that "for the purpose of salvation the most important thing is <u>*obedience to the teachings of Jesus Christ,*</u> *and everything else is secondary or of little importance.*" So it is well if one understands that God is only one in essence and in person; however, if one understands and believes this, and is disobedient to the teaching of Jesus, *the correct belief is worthless.*

So if you believe the common Christian belief in the Trinity is in error, what do you believe is a correct belief concerning Jesus Christ, the Son of God?

I will respond to that later. Let me just say at this point the *nature of Jesus Christ is indeed separate from God,* and common Trinitarian beliefs on this subject are in error!

Okay then, that still leaves us with the question of the *Holy Spirit,* who is believed to be one with the Father and Son. Since you say that Trinitarian beliefs are groundless in the holy word, *what then should we believe about the Holy Spirit?*

The word spirit (spiritus in Latin) in itself means the force or energy to do something; the Holy Spirit is simply the force, or spirit of God, that from God's own sanctity, accomplishes something.

Can you support this idea from the holy word?

Yes.

In the final chapter of Luke (24:49) "quoadusque induami virtute ex alto," (until you are endowed with Virtue from on High), the idea here of *Highest Virtue* is synonymous with *The Holy Spirit.* This same *Highest Virtue* would be given to the Apostle Paul (Luke 1:35). Otherwise we could simply say here that Paul received the *Holy Spirit.*

Even if we go along with this rather oblique argument, how do you reconcile the fact that in the holy word, the Holy Spirit is called a person? How could the Holy Spirit be separate and yet one with God?

Often in the Bible (Jam. 3:17, Rom. 7:8 &c, Joh.3:8) *metaphorical language is used.* It is the same with the idea of the force of God being *personified.* *Thus the Holy Spirit is not a separate person, only the force of God.*

Again, how important are these beliefs to our eternal well-being?

These beliefs are *extremely important because the truth is always important,* and especially so when it comes *directly from Jesus, the father of Glory.*

Do you have any more to say about *divine essence?*

No! We need to understand *salvation* is ultimately from God, so that we can be *obedient to Jesus Christ!*

Then if salvation is from God, shouldn't we understand the *nature of God* as it pertains to his goodness?

Yes, and with that beneficence, perfect honesty and equality. Further, even though the goodness of God is *beyond our ability* to comprehend, we can understand that *God's goodness is voluntary,* and the *will of God* stems from that *voluntary goodness.*

WILL OF GOD

So what can we understand about the *will of God?*

The will of God (as it relates to our human history) is God's works, teachings, and decrees that show us the way to eternal salvation.

So how is *human history* connected to the *will of God?*

It is through the Creation (Gen. 1), the life of *individual humans* (Gen. 18:25), and the possibility of salvation for those who *obey his laws* (Heb. 11:16).

So what you are saying is that for our salvation we must believe *God made the universe?*

Yes, of course! We should believe that God is the *author of the universe,* because God commands us to believe it, and because without the promise of *God's love* for each person, there is no solid foundation for *morality.*

Almost the entirety of humanity believes that God created the universe and bases their moral existence on this precept. Ultimately, is this as much as we need to know for a *solid foundation of morality?*

No! To understand *morality, completely* and the *goals of morality* we <u>must</u> do our best to understand Jesus Christ!

JESUS CHRIST

In order to *strengthen our morals,* what should we understand about Jesus Christ?

Jesus teaches us the will of God so that we can be *obedient,* and with that *obedience,* receive the benefits of the promises made to us.

You have made a major point of the fact that the *nature of God* and *Jesus* are *separate,* so how does understanding the *separate nature of Jesus* help us attain the goal of obedience to God?

That's difficult to answer, but just let me say, at this point, that the *will of God* was revealed to Jesus by God and was not of the nature of Jesus. Or to say this in another way, *during his life Jesus performed the work of God*.

Are you saying that the *will of God* is separate from the *nature of Jesus Christ?*

Yes, I am. Jesus Christ holds the *divine power, i.e., holy spirit* within us (Rom. 14:9), and he has *supreme majesty* over us (Ephes. 1:20), beyond anything possible to imagine, in *majesty* with God himself (1Cor. 15:27, Phil. 2:8&9, and Hebr. 2:9), not from his own *nature*, but endowed with power from God because of his *obedience*, even unto his *death on the cross* and *resurrection.*

If I understand you correctly, what you are saying comes out in the end like the beliefs in traditional Christianity i.e., *Jesus Christ is divine.* So why do we need to understand Jesus as having a *separate nature from God?*

Yes, because the purpose of the *divinity of Jesus Christ* is to establish the *will of God* in *humanity* (John 5:23, Psalm. 45:12, Hebr. 1:6, and Phil. 2:10). He is to care for *his own kind*, meaning his *own kind of human nature.* Through our *humanity* we can better understand the *will of God* while at the same time we can revere God independently in nature from *Jesus as the pure source of our ideals.*

THE NATURE OF JESUS CHRIST

So how do you explain the *nature of Jesus Christ* as *different from that of God?*

The nature of Jesus Christ is Human to the extent that he was *born of the Virgin Mary* from the power of the *Holy Spirit* (Math.

1:20&23, Luke 1:35), thus he started his life with the *weakness and mortality shared by all humans* (2Cor. 13:4). Then he went into the world by the command of God and fulfilled his mission. *It was <u>after</u> Jesus had fulfilled his mission that he ascended to heaven and was made divine with absolute power and immortality (Rom. 6:9).*

I can't help but notice that you avoid saying, *"Jesus is the eternal most high, only begotten son of the father"* (Rom. 8:32, John 1:14 &18). Why?

I have mentioned that Jesus Christ is the *"only begotten son of God"* in discussing the *nature of Jesus Christ.*

I remain unconvinced! So please tell me why would God call Jesus his: *"only begotten son"*, if *Jesus is of another nature?*

Okay let me reiterate this one more time, to explain what I mean. *Jesus Christ was born of the Virgin Mary by the power of God, i.e., the Holy Spirit.* Thus, he is called *"the son of God"* (Luke 1:35). Now it follows that the *son of God* is *individual* and *only begotten from God,* but as I mentioned, *"the miracle of the virgin birth of Jesus was accomplished through the power of god,"* and this essentially says more about the relationship between *Jesus Christ* and *God* than merely stating *Jesus Christ* is the *only begotten son of God!* The words, *"Jesus Christ the only begotten son of God"* can be *misunderstood easily.*

Maybe it is me, but I find this answer still lacking. Please, narrow this answer down, so I can understand it. Why is Jesus Christ called the *"only begotten son of God,"* if his *nature is <u>different</u>* from the nature of God?

Let's take a look at the name Jesus Christ. Nowhere in the Bible where we read *"Jesus Christ, the son of God,"* does it simply say *Christ*, but always *Jesus Christ* (Acts. 3:13, I Thess. 1:10, Hebr. 4:14).

All right, so how do you explain this?

Because the name Jesus is a personal human name that is used to *signify the humanity of Christ* (Math 1:13& Math. 1:16), while the name *Christ* is used to *signify the relation of Jesus to God as savior and king. When Christ appears by itself, it refers to the humanity of Jesus that has added the authority of God.*

So how do you define this *independent authority*?

I define this *authority* as the authority given to Jesus Christ in order to *rule the people of God by divine ordination* (I Sam. 8:9 & 10). It was the same type of ordination that was used in the ordination of the *kings of Israel.* Thus, the name Christ means: *"called and ordained by God".*

You have limited the meaning of the "only begotten son of God, Jesus Christ," to the humanity of Jesus and power given by God, so in effect, we are not freed from our sins or given eternal life by Jesus Christ as God, so what is left in the meaning of Christ?

The name Jesus Christ only means he is an *individual* and also a *king.*

How have you deduced this limited view?

I have drawn this belief from the reality that Jesus Christ is the *individual origin of the people of God,* as their *absolute king.* There has never been, nor is it possible, for there to ever be another *absolute king* like Jesus.

Why is that?

Because Jesus has *absolute power* which no earthly king has had. Earthly kings are plagued by being unable to punish insurrections and assassinations. Often they are powerless to help their own subjects. *The power of earthly kings is external* while Jesus, in his *absolute power, has power over things of the spirit.*

Weren't the *children of Israel* within the *absolute realm and power of God?*

No. Only the very *just and god-fearing Israelites* were in the *realm of God.* The children of Israel for the most part were not *just or god-fearing.*

Why were they called *the children of God* then?

It is because God chose them for his own, in order to reveal his *will and judgment* (Psalms 147: 19&20).

So how do we compare the kingdoms established by God in the Old Testament and the realm of Jesus?

The *kingdoms of Israel* cannot be compared with the *kingdom of Jesus* because the *kingdoms of Israel* were comprised of people whose faith was questionable, the *kings of Israel* did not have *absolute power,* and their hold on the power that they had was *tenuous at best.* Therefore, when we say, *"Jesus Christ, the* only *begotten son of God,"* we are setting the *kingdom of Jesus Christ* apart from all other kingdoms.

This all seems very obvious without using the name of *Jesus Christ* to explain it! Couldn't other ways be employed to explain the title *"Jesus Christ, the only begotten son of God?"*

Certainly, if we think of the *exercising of judgment,* we can see that Jesus Christ is our *ultimate judge* because he is the *"only begotten anointed son of God."* This title also sets him apart in time; *i.e.,* there could be no other before or after Jesus that could compare in judgment with him.

Then I have to ask you, what about the understanding in traditional Christianity that Jesus is called the "only begotten son of God" because he is generated of the same substance as God?

I believe this idea has evolved simply as a convention of speech, and that there is virtually no scriptural support for it. I also believe this idea to be contrary to clear thinking. *Or, would God generate from his own substance that which was corruptible, and at the same time, hold that as part of him, and yet divided? Jesus Christ is the individual son of God born of the Virgin Mary, as is testified to by the Holy Scriptures (Math. 16:16, Mark 8:29, Luke 9:20, Math. 26:63, Mark14:61, Luke 22:67&69, John 20:31).* So the *historical reality* is that Jesus became the absolute king of God's people **AFTER** his resurrection and was established as the divine son and of God's own kind *through resurrection from the dead* (Rom. 1:4, Acts. 13:13). So it is that when we look at the original Greek in <u>The Book of Romans,</u> the Greek word οριοθεντος *(designated)* is used to indicate the *historical point* at which *Jesus Christ* was made the *absolute perfect king of his people.*

I must say that you have carefully avoided the many places in the holy word where Jesus Christ is called "God." Don't all of these references indicate that Jesus Christ is of the *same substance and essence as God?*

I admit I have made no express mention of these citations, but didn't I cover this in a fashion in the discussion of the meaning of the name Christ?   Also, I did discuss the reason that the essence of Jesus and God must be seen as separate, because what can we possibly understand of the *nature of Jesus Christ if his nature is so clearly alien from ours, and how can we ever get a feeling of kinship with Jesus from the idea that the substance of Jesus Christ was generated from God?*

This answer is not satisfactory. You need to address my question, by discussing the scriptures where *Jesus Christ is called God.*

Alright then, *Jesus Christ is called God because of the power and majesty that he holds within us (John 1:1 & 20:21).* Further, the *title God* does not refer to *essence or substance.* Even the mentally challenged can figure out that the *name God* refers to *authority and power*, and not *essence or substance.* In the Hebrew and the Greek, the appellation of God is translated as one of *authority and power! So it is that the angels are endowed with the power of God (2 Peter 2:11).* And so it is with us humans, when we grant authority, we say, *"in the name of God," "go with God,"* or *"in God's speed,"* etc. We can read about the testimony of *God's power* as it relates to *Angels* (Psalms 8 & 97), explained also in the letter to the Hebrews 1&2. By comparison, we can understand the *power of humans* as it is outlined in Exodus 21:6 22:8 and 28. And, we read in Psalms 82 "Ego dixi dii est" (I said he is from God), which is the same as Jesus himself said, *"he was from God,* and that he *by himself, he was not God, but the Son of God"* (John 10). *However, we can say that Jesus is like God in the sense that the God of Gods named him in Deut. 10, sanctified him and sent him into the world.*

If Jesus is not strictly speaking as God, (as you believe), what should we take this phrase, *"He was sanctified and sent into the world,"* to mean?

"Sanctification" means that he was always full of the *Holy Spirit, excellent and sublime.* He was also *separated* from the things of this world. The meaning of *"sent into the world"* is that Jesus was *commissioned by God* for his mission in the same way that Jesus *commissioned his apostles for theirs.* And let me add, these things need to be understood historically; i.e., *they occurred at a point in time* as part of the *historical social reality* (John 17:18). So *Jesus Christ can be called God, but he was not made from the substance of God.* The reason I would like you to understand this is that a correct understanding puts the emphasis on the *humanity of the God, Jesus Christ,* so we can better understand the importance of *divine power* and how it pertains to *good works.*

What does this mean for all of the *good people* who have misunderstood and *held on fiercely to* the idea that *Jesus was generated out of the substance of God?*

The main thing (as I have said before) is to be *obedient to the teachings of Jesus Christ.* As long as they are obedient and exercise charity to those who do not share their views; i.e., they do not teach that those others (who believe as we do) are opponents that need to be persecuted, then these erroneous beliefs will not hinder their eternal well-being.

Well then, should one proclaim correct beliefs, or just leave well enough alone?

Certainly correct beliefs should be proclaimed. First of all, because a correct *understanding of the human nature of Jesus Christ exalts our own human nature,* and motivates us to accomplish the work we are given by the *Divine Power of God. What is most quintessential in this is to strive toward faith and hope in our God* (I Peter 1:3 & 21, & Chapter 3:21 &22, Hebr. 4:5 &16)! *Striving toward a Faith and Hope in our God is the message set forth by all of God's prophets.*

So are you teaching that human nature is in the exaltation of Jesus Christ?

Yes! We need to understand this because without this understanding, we cannot understand *Christ's Divine Church. Further, we need to understand that the Divine Power of Jesus Christ is part of our human condition!*

THE DIVINE POWER OF JESUS CHRIST

What is the meaning of the *majesty of Jesus Christ* as his *majesty* relates to *Divine Power?*

The majesty of Jesus is that he is the king of the true people of God. Jesus is the *"only begotten son of God"* who by his *obedience to his father, has become the Christ.*

So can you please tell me more about *Divine Power?*

Jesus has *power over all angels and spirits,* and the evil ones as well as the good.

How does he exercise this power over the good angels and spirits?

He leads the good *angels and spirits* to support the *God-fearing and pious* in their striving for *eternal well-being.*

That makes sense, but *what power does he exercise over evil?*

Jesus knows his own, and when the honest and just are threatened, he will use his power to strengthen them internally, so that they can withstand the trials that are placed before them. Also, Jesus, on certain occasions, uses his power to liberate his people from the power of evil. He uses his power to ostracize the unjust and evil from his own. Thus, the power of Jesus tends to his glory.

So what you are saying then, is that, in reality, *Jesus has absolute power over all of humanity?*

Yes, but Jesus *holds this power in unity with God* (I Cor. 15:27). And let's understand here, when I say *unity,* I mean *unity* of *purpose and design, not substance. Also, from the reality of the separate nature of God and Jesus, we can deduce that ultimately God has more power than Jesus.*

So who has power over *death and hell*?

Certainly, Jesus holds power over death and hell, for otherwise, how could he free the *true people of God.* Or, so it is written, *"He holds the keys of death and hell"* (Rev. 1:18).

Doesn't this bring us to the necessity of the *resurrection of Jesus Christ?*

Yes, and to validate the resurrection, humans had to bear witness of it. As the Apostle Paul taught, *"without the resurrection of Jesus Christ from death, our faith is inane"* (I Cor. 15:14 & c.).

Shouldn't we believe because of the resurrection, *Jesus is living right now?*

Yes, because death is *unable to hold dominion over him* (Rom. 6:9).

Let me ask you this then. *When we pray, in effect, are we only praying to Jesus?*

Yes, because as a gift from God, Jesus is our absolute king. This is especially true because Christ came to be our king through obedience within the human experience; i.e., God has given us to Jesus to be part of his kingdom, because Jesus knows our hearts (Rev. 2:23).

So what about all of those who don't hold these beliefs?

If they do *not believe Jesus is the Christ, they are not Christians.*

REJECTION OF THE BELIEFS OF THE ARIANS

How do can you support your beliefs when it is well understood (by the vast majority of Christians) that Jesus existed in substance prior to the Virgin Birth?

First, let me respond by saying *Jesus Christ is human in nature. Human because to the natives of this life of suffering and affliction, he came <u>as one of us</u> to relieve our suffering and lead us to eternal life.* And, I must say your question seems out of place because we have already gone over this at length!

Surely you can see my confusion here. Jesus is taught by you to be one of us, *yet in so many ways superior!* Please tell me plainly, *how is he like us?*

Jesus being of our nature, experienced the same temptations as the rest of us (Heb. 4:15), and from those experiences he not only was able to remain without guilt, but is better able to lead us from a life of sin. Let's approach this human nature question another way: let's analyze the idea of resurrection. It says in (1 Cor. 15:13 & 16.) "Si resurrection mortuorum non est, nec Chistus resurrexit", *(If there is no resurrection, then Christ was not resurrected). We know there is a resurrection because of the reality of the resurrection of Jesus as testified to by the witnesses, but what does that mean? If Jesus Christ by resurrection became something more excellent than anything human, how can those of a human nature share in the resurrection,* or to put this yet another way, *how does our human experience relate to the resurrection, and how can the promises that were made to us by God, based on our human experience and nature, mean anything?*

Are your teachings like the followers of Arius who also teach that Jesus was human in nature, while maintaining that Jesus lived before he was born of the Virgin?

No! Nothing that is singular can be plural at the same time. One is one, not two. Jesus was and always will be "The only begotten son of God," i.e., one. The Arians support their teachings by saying that Jesus had an *eternal essence*; i.e., Jesus existed in a perfect state before he was born. Then he adopted a human nature as a vestment. Other Christians teach that Jesus is one in substance with God the father. *Even though both of these teachings arrive at Jesus adopting a human form, his essence and beginning are <u>not</u> human, meaning that ultimately the reality of Jesus becomes estranged from our human condition and nature.*

Aren't the teachings of the Arians in conflict with the teachings of those in Christianity who teach that Jesus is of the same substance as God?

Yes, and we don't agree with either one of them! We find the belief that God and Jesus are of the same substance and number to be the more pernicious, but we can't accept either belief. The Arians explain the birth of Jesus as a spontaneous event born of necessity, and even though they teach that Jesus has a human nature, if he sprang from an eternal essence unlike anything of humanity, we must ask, how could this be?

How can the Arians believe that Jesus was born of his own spontaneity, when in the holy word in so many places, he is called the "son of man"?

The Arians do not believe that where it is written in the Bible the "son of man," the word man should be taken literally, but rather to mean "the human Christ is of his own generation new and heavenly." We cannot accept these beliefs because, as I have said, the Apostle Paul, in the Holy Scriptures, clearly says: "that Jesus was made immortal and glorified" (I Cor. 15:47), as he says: "Adam was the first earthly human and Christ, the second heavenly human." In summary, we believe as Paul taught, we, like Jesus, start with an earthly body that can be made heavenly (Phil.3:2I).

I can see how the teachings of the Arians are in contradiction. If Jesus was only human, how could he have lived before his human existence? On the other hand, though, how do you explain (because you too believe the nature of Christ to be *only human*), that in the Holy Scriptures it is written (John 1:3-10 &

Colossians. 1:16) *"that the world and everything in it was made through Jesus?"*

Let me say first that there are few words in the Bible used more frequently than "Omni (*everything*)." When we read "everything," we are not to take it as a *universal*, but the meaning should be put in context. So in John 1:3, *John is talking about the gospel.* If you would like to understand the way everything can be used where it does not mean <u>everything</u>, just look at 2nd Cor. 5:17, where Paul says, *"Everything was made new,"* and clearly *not every little thing in the world became new!*

Even if, I go along with your rather limited reasoning here, how do you explain the passage in John where it clearly states *"without the word, i.e., Jesus Christ the son of God, nothing was made, since clearly here, there was an extreme effort to put <u>no limit on the idea of "everything"</u>?*

What was meant in this place was that without the "Word" *(the Gospel)*, nothing could have been made *new* and *marvelous*; *i.e., without Jesus, we have no "word," or no "gospel,"* and the *"old order of Moses"* would <u>not</u> *have been replaced with the new and marvelous gospel of Jesus Christ!* The best example of the way **All THINGS** (in this context) were impossible to accomplish without Jesus, is if we think of how *dependent* all of the *marvelous works* of the Apostles were *on Jesus* (John 15:5) "Sine me nihil potestis facere (without me, you can do nothing)".

Again your reasoning seems shallow! Both in John and in Paul it is stated (John 1:10), "the world was made through the son of God," so why would they preach this way, if you are correct?

In this same chapter, the word *"world"* is used three times, and always the meaning is *figurative*. We can see this *figurative usage in:* **Jesus is of the World (John 4:42), and** *Jesus is the* *bread that gives life to the World* **(I John 6:33).** *When we say* *someone is born, isn't a figurative form of speech that means we* *experience an event that gives life?* **In Hebrew, compound words do not exist, so often what should have been written as** *"remade"* *would have been written as "made".* **If we substitute** *"remade"* **for made in this scripture, and realized that the word** *"world"* **means** *humankind,* **the meaning becomes clear;** *Jesus came to* *reform humankind. So, when we read, "Jesus came to the world* *and the world knew him not," or "Jesus came to save the world,"* *this is not in reference to the planet Earth. These uses are* *figurative and need to be understood in context.* **If we think of** *"world"* **meaning strictly the** *"planet"* **that we live on, these scriptures where the word** *"world"* **is used would become** *nonsensical; i.e., the planet Earth was made in the form of Jesus* *Christ, the planet Earth rejected Jesus etc.*

If I go along with what you are saying, *and I am not saying that I* *do,* **how would you interpret the word** *"world"* **in these passages?**

I am saying that we need to understand the context of what is *being said, and the limitations on written word,* **or** *if we put the* *same meaning everywhere to a word that is used figuratively, we* *can wind up with some serious misunderstandings.* **So, let me go over what I believe are correct understandings of the word** *World* **in these passages. In the first case where it says "Jesus came to the world," the meaning of the word** *world* **is** *human civilization* *on Earth.* **Where it says, "Through Jesus Christ the** *world* **was made", the meaning of the word** *world* **is that Jesus would establish the possibility of a** *future eternal world* **for his followers (which of course is the present world for Jesus and his angels); i.e., the meaning here to a great extent deals with the subject of** *time.* And, finally, where it says *"and the world did not know him,"* the meaning is that *carnal humans,* with their weaknesses and *faults,* did not know him, *and rejected him.*

The first and third interpretations of the word *"world"* seem all right, and can be supported in the holy word, *but that middle one is a reach; how did you come by it?*

I admit talking about *time in a simultaneous way is something new, and maybe a little confusing.* However, in one Letter to the Hebrews, we can see the beginning of the *order of Jesus Christ* in a *historical sense,* and also his *eternal order.* (Heb. 1:6) "Cum iterum introductit progenitum in orbem terrae, dicit, & adorent eum omnes Angeli Dei" *(When he presents the first born to the world, he says, let all of the angels of God pay him homage).* For here we can see the beginning of the *order of Christ* as an event in the *history of the world,* because both in the Latin: "Orbis Terrae (Planet Earth) and Greek Οικουμενης (inhabited world)," the meanings of the word *"world"* are nearly the same, i.e., *our planet, and our planet's history.*

Okay, but again, isn't it a bit of a reach to derive the meaning of a future eternal order from this passage?

Yes, maybe, but with these additional passages, I will make this idea clear (Psalms 97 & Hebr. 1:6). First we read in Psalms 97, *"The Lord is king; let the earth rejoice; let the many islands be glad. Cloud and darkness surround the Lord: justice and right are the foundation of his throne. Fire goes before him: everywhere it consumes the foes. Lightning illumines the world; the earth sees and trembles. The mountains melt like wax before the Lord, before the Lord of all the earth. The heavens proclaim God's justice; all peoples see his glory. All who serve idols are put to shame, who glory in worthless things; all gods bow down before you. Zion hears and is glad, and the cities of Judah rejoice because of your judgments, O Lord. You, Lord, are the Most High over all the earth, exalted far above all gods. The Lord loves those who hate evil, protects the lives of the faithful, rescues them from the hand of the wicked. Light dawns for the just; gladness, for the honest of heart. Rejoice in the Lord, you just and praise his holy name,"* Now, we compare this passage with **Hebrews 1:6, "And again, when he leads the first-born into the world, he says: Let all of the angels of God worship him."[12]**

I can see how one can compare these passages; however how have you arrived at the conclusion that they both are speaking of a future world ruled by Jesus Christ?

These passages are connected by the adoration of Christ by angels. The future eternal world is spoken of in time: i.e. after Christ's mission on Earth is complete.

I still find all of this hard to see as you would like me to! Do you have more to add?

Two ideas should make the meaning of a *future world* abundantly clear! When Jesus walked the earth, he did not have power over all of the angels. *He was given that power after his death on the Cross (Eph. 1:20 &c., Philipp. 2:8 & c., I Peter 3:22). And let me add, the adoration by heavenly hosts was because of the obedience of Jesus even unto death; i.e., again we see necessary historical events and sequence here! In Philippians, the testimony is most clear; that Jesus Christ was to be exalted above all <u>because</u> of his obedience even unto his death on the cross.*

I have to question how this reference in Psalms (Psalms 97) fits your argument. How do we know the *"world"* referred to here is a *future world?*

Primarily because Psalms 97 is prophetic material about Jesus obtaining his kingdom, after his life on Earth was through. Then crowned in glory because he overcame death through his obedient life, death on the cross and resurrection (Luke 24:26, I Peter 1:11, Hebr.2:9).

Even if I accept this, how do you interpret the usage of the word *"world"* in Hebrews to mean the *future world of Christ's kingdom?*

In Hebrews, the ideas expressed are about the organization of Christ's kingdom (Hebr. 2:5). The Latin and Greek words for world refer to the inhabited kingdom of Christ, so even though a strict interpretation of the word "world" by itself does not yield the idea of a future kingdom of Christ, we can infer this meaning from the context of the discussion. In Paul, we read (Paul 1:6), "per quem fecit et saecula, (through whom the ages are made)." *Clearly this refers to time to come.*

Is there another specific reference in the writings of Paul that supports your contention, *because I can't agree that Paul 1:6 is referring to a future time?*

Yes, in Chapter 10 vs. 5 we read; "ingrediens mundum dicit, hostiam et oblationem noluisti, corpus autem aptasti mihi, &c", (by coming into the world, sacrifice as offerings are done away with, you have prepared a body for me). Again here, we see a reference to the new order of Jesus Christ of the future, i.e., a time after the old order of sacrifice of animals, when the resurrected Jesus comes into his own kingdom. Thus it is in King

David's fortieth psalm that he foretells of his own liberation by Jesus. These same ideas are repeated by the Apostle Peter (Acts 2:24, 31 &33). *These scriptures are about the glorious future world where we are free from the effects of sin and can live in happy immortality with Jesus. And so it is, that Christ ascending into heaven becomes our eternal high priest (Hebr. 5:9-10, 7:26, 8:2 & 9:20).*

Wait a minute here! *You have just managed to contradict everything you have said about the beginning of Jesus Christ! The Latin "corpus autem aptasti mihi" (you have prepared a body for me), illustrates two things very clearly that contradict what you have said about the beginning of Jesus Christ and his nature. If a body was prepared, it would certainly follow that Jesus lived before the body was prepared, which supports the traditional Christian view that Jesus is eternal and one with God!* So how can you explain the contradiction in your belief?

I could have translated "aptasti" in *other ways* which would also be valid, i.e., *you apposite, or you conjoined.* It could also be said that *"you produced, you composed or you completed,"* would work as well for they are valid synonyms, but I am going to stand by the way I have translated "aptasti," because the Greek Καταστησει should be translated *"you make."*

Aren't you just digging yourself a deeper hole here?

No! I will explain. *The proper meaning here is that God produced the possibility for the body of Christ to come into blessed immortality, i.e., God's gift of immortality that frees us from the old order of sacrificial victims, and replaces it with Jesus as the sole eternal sacrificial victim (Hebr. 7:16 & 28, & Chapter 9 vs. 14).* As a parallel example to what is written in Second Hebrews, we read in Psalms 40, "aur e perfodisti mihi" (my ears you opened). And now I think it is time for me to address your questions about the Apostle Paul who wrote, *"through Jesus Christ everything was created."*

You will find that I am patient! First, though, I would like you to try to clear something up. In Hebrews I:2 & 1:27, it clearly states by the use of "Saeculum & Mundum" (ages and world) *together,* that there is to be no confusion with the idea that the word *"world"* is limited, i.e., *to mean the future world, or new order of Jesus Christ, but rather the planet Earth and time as is believed by Christians everywhere!*

I am not going to argue that "Saeculum" means *ages or time,* nor am I going to doubt that you are correct about the beliefs of the *majority of Christians.* Just let me say first, I doubt that anyone would dispute that "Saeculum" *(time)* would not include <u>future time</u>. The two locations that you cite are in separate locations, and "Saeculum" *(time)* can have very different meanings according to the context. "Saeculum," can be used to mean time, ages, worlds, periods, etc. Even if we accept that "Saeculum" can be plugged in to have the same meaning in all of these locations, that doesn't mean we should do it! Another meaning for "Saeculum" is <u>Eternity</u> (Math. 6:11&13). *Often in the New Testament, "Saeculum" is translated to mean (all eternity or forever) (Rom. 1:25, 9:5, 11:36, 16:27, 2 Cor. 11:31). The Latin is translated from the Greek* αιωνας *(age, or eternal time), and the Greek word has many more meanings than this (present world).*

So, when we translate "Saecula" as "world," shouldn't the connected *time significance* be more than our *normal Earth time?*

Of course! So in the beginning of the letter to the Hebrews, the Apostle Paul is speaking of the son of God (Jesus of Nazareth), who would appear at the end of the days of the prophets, to establish the future world, with the possibility of eternal life for humans. *This was all done through the earthly life of Jesus Christ (son of God), and not before (2 Peter 3:13).*

Okay, your arguments are clear enough for anyone to understand your beliefs on the issue of the creation of the *world* or *time* by Jesus. I remain unconvinced, because of all of those places in the holy word where it says that through Jesus *all things* were created. *How can you deny that Jesus is our Creator?*

You are talking about (Eph. 3:9) and (Colossians. 1:16), in both these locations it states: *"All things were made through Jesus Christ."* However, the Greek translation differs from the Latin and Syrian. But we need not get into *semantics* on this issue because we can understand what was meant by understanding the message of the Apostle Paul. Clearly in the letter to the Ephesians the Apostle Paul does not want us to understand that the word "Omnia" (Everything) should be taken to mean literally *"Everything" in the universe, but rather "everything" within the second creation, or the reformation through Jesus Christ. He is talking about how all things are made new through Jesus.* For example, *the way the Jews and Gentiles become one people through Jesus. Certainly, in the fulfillment of promises of the law of love Jesus makes everything new according to Paul.* That is why Paul says: "before Christ, these things were a mystery" (Ephes. 3:4 & c), the "mystery" being the establishment of the possibility of *Eternal Life* (Rom. 16:25). *When Paul talks about everything here, he is talking about the order of God, and how* that order was reformed by God through Jesus Christ, or _made new_ (*2 Cor. 5:17*).

With all you have said, I still remain _very_ skeptical because in other testimonies it clearly states: *all things in Heaven, and on Earth, the visible, and the invisible!*

Okay, let's use a little bit of reason to get through this! Paul writes a little further on: *"Through the crucifixion and blood of Christ, peace was made with all things on Earth, and in heaven (Colossians 1).* Yet, unless we are blind we understand that this cannot be! *Can rocks still fall on us? Can we still be struck by lightning? How about the devil? This pacification applies to humans and angels (in heaven and on earth) endowed with higher intelligence. Now, some might argue that the devil is neither of heaven or earth, but I really don't have time to deal with that!*

Are you saying that the angels needed to be brought in harmony with God through the crucifixion and blood of Christ because of sin?

You should be able to figure this out from what I have already said, but pacification has more than one side to it, the angels who were always in harmony with God had become discordant with humans after the fall of Adam. What this holy passage is referring to is the beginning of Christ's reign of glory, and his church. *Through the crucifixion and blood of Christ, angels are brought in harmony with mankind (2 Cor. 5:19 & Rom. 5:10).* The centrality of Jesus to this pacification is clearer in the Greek and Syrian versions of the Bible because there it says "through Christ himself."

Now we have another problem with your beliefs! How is it that thrones, dominations, powers, etc., are reformed through Christ?

Angels are included in these designations, but in a general way. These designations are talking about divisions in the spirit world, i.e., divisions between angels, and both good and evil spirits (**1Peter 3:22**). Later on I will talk about the way Paul makes distinctions in these matters, but for now, just let me say that in Romans 8:38, *Paul distinguishes angels from principalities.*

I am very unclear about all of this, if we are not talking primarily about angels here, what are we talking about?

We are talking about the *evil spirits* that dominate our *present wicked world,* as the Apostle Paul describes in Ephesians 6:12.

Well then, how are *angels, good spirits and evil spirits all reformed through Jesus Christ?*

This became possible because Jesus Christ was made absolute in his Power as Paul describes in his letters to Ephesians and Colossians. Further, in these letters we can see how the angels are distinguished from powers and virtues.

In order to get a better grasp of what you have said, *is it worthwhile to compare Paul's letters to the Ephesians with the letters to the Colossians?*

Yes, because the letters to the Ephesians and Colossians closely correspond, and in places can be tied together; for example begin at Colossians 2:10, then compare Ephesians 1:21, *Colossians 2:10: "and you share in this fullness in him, who is the head of every principality and power",* then Ephesians: 1:21 *"far above every principality, authority, power, and dominion, and every name that is named not only in this age, but also in the one to come."*[13] These passages help us understand, that at the beginning of Christ's reign, Jesus sits in glory on the right hand of God with power over all that is in heaven and earth!

I still find your explanations somewhat unsatisfactory. Can one find any other places in the holy word that support your belief that these passages are about a *secondary creation* rather than a *primary creation?*

It is hard to believe that one word can cause such great misunderstanding, but when the Hebrew language was translated without compounding create to be re-create, we have inherited a great deal of confusion. If we look at the whole of the Gospel, we can see plainly that we are God's workmanship made through Jesus Christ (Ephesians 2:10 "ipuius enim (Dei) sumus facture, create in Christo Jesu," & c. truly we are his (God's) workmanship created through Jesus Christ). In many places in the Bible, the understanding would have been better if the passages read "formed and reformed" rather than simply "created" (Zech. 2:11 & Eph. 2:10).

If there is confusion here, it is because you have *confused* what is plainly true in the Bible concerning the role Jesus played in the original creation. *Before the quotation that you cite in Colossians, it clearly states that Jesus Christ was the first of all creatures.* Now if Christ was the first of all creatures, isn't reasonable to believe that he was the original creator?

Of course not! *The word "creature" has the same problem here as "create"; before it, it should have been written "new creatures," instead of "creatures."* This idea is made clear in James 1:18, where from the Greek, we read "Of his own will he made us with the word of truth, so that we would be the particular first fruits of his labor; *i.e., Jesus is the first of his new creatures*. The word "creature" was translated in blanket fashion. Sometimes the sense should be "new creature," and sometimes, it just means "creature" as in Romans 8:19 & c. *We need to look at the context of the scriptures to understand the proper meaning.*

Aren't you *degrading the Glory of Christ* by counting him only among the *"new creatures of God"*?

I see what you are saying here. If we only count Jesus among the "new creatures of God," then where he is called the "primogenitor," we would also need to say that he was created. As Of course if we say that, we cannot contend that he always existed. Then if we say that Jesus Christ is a creature like the rest of us, people would have a more difficult time believing in the resurrection of Jesus Christ, or his immortality and glory.

Certainly that is a great concern! And yet, if we follow this line of thinking, wouldn't it follow that Jesus, as the first of the new creatures, was also the first to be transformed from *death into* blessed immortality?

*Yes, in a way we could say that, but we must be *careful* here because there are necessary differences between Jesus, the first of all new creatures, and other of the new creatures! Jesus, unlike other new creatures was conceived by the power of the Holy Spirit, i.e. he was in no way conceived through the normal human reproductive process, but by the virtue of God. Further, unlike the rest of humanity, Jesus led a life without sin. In John 1:13, it clearly states, "the new creatures are not born of the blood, flesh or will of man, but are of God." So, after the* *transformation into eternal life, the new creatures are in no way connected with sin (1st John3:6, 8&9).*

Because of the *profound nature* of these discussions of Christ and the new creatures in the Bible, would you say we should not get carried away with *being literal?*

Yes, I would. *There is a lot of mystery in this area of theology, and we have a difficult time understanding the similarities, and differences between Jesus and other new creatures.*

From what I have seen of your approach to the holy word, you must have some logic to support your belief in a second creation?

Yes, I do. *The Apostle Paul is constantly saying our redemption is in and through Jesus (Ephesians 1:7 "per sanguine eius" (through his blood). So let me ask you; how do we connect to Jesus Christ in this intimate way, if we are not one in nature with him?* Further, concerning those creation references in the writings of Paul, if the Apostle Paul had meant the primal creation, *why wouldn't he mention one little fish or animal, or any of the other things that were part of the primal creation described in the Old Testament* (Gen. 2:4, 2 Kings 19:15, 2 Chron. 2:12, Psalms 102:26 & 115, Isaiah 37:16)?

How can you believe this when it clearly states in the Bible, *"In the beginning was the word, and the word was with God,"* when the "word" in these references (2 Peter 3:5, John 1:1, Revelations19:13 with Psalms 33:6) is Jesus the Christ?

Yes, the Son of God could be said to be the "word" of God. The "word" of God mentioned in these locations does not necessarily mean the same thing! The "word" associated with primal creation refers to the decrees and orders of God that made the primal creation possible. *We have to look at what the "word" of God accomplishes; i.e., "Let there be dry land etc".* Because of limitations in verb usage in Hebrew and their translations, i.e., the idea of "bearing forth" or "declaring" can wind up as the "original word." When we go to the New Testament, we don't find the usage of the "word" in connection with primal creation, *but rather the usage speaks of the mediation of Jesus Christ by the power of God.*

You have said that the Son of God can be understood to be the "word," and yet you seem to take the important significance out of the meaning, so tell me what significance do you give to Jesus Christ as the "word"?

Jesus is the "word" because he helps us to understand God (John 1:18), "Deum nemo vidit uqquam: unigenitus filius, qui est in sinu patris ipse enarravit" (nobody has ever seen God; it is the only begotten son who is in the bosom of the father; he himself hath taught us about him). The evangelist Paul calls Jesus the "word," because it is *through Jesus we understand the will and council of God.*

I find it real surprising that you quote John, because in the Book of John, *it is clear that there is <u>nothing</u> before or above Jesus Christ. Don't these scriptures seem nonsensical, if Jesus is only human in nature?*

We have already covered this subject at length (in the meaning of the name Jesus Christ)! However, I can add: Jesus spoke of God as the "word," and it is in this sense of the "word," the idea is held of <u>nothing before</u> or <u>above</u> God himself. *Concerning the humanity of Jesus, when Jesus spoke of God objectively as the "word," he was declaring his own individuality and humanity!*

A grammatical deduction proves nothing! Can you show me anything in the Book of John that proves Jesus is only human in nature?

If we understand the holy word to teach that Jesus Christ is the original creator of <u>everything</u> then it is certainly unclear how his nature could be only human, but I would hope we have dispelled this myth. It says in the Gospel of John, "He came to his own, and his own knew him not," and of course, <u>his own are human</u>. But we have gone over all of this, so let me add that the Apostle John himself called Jesus a <u>man</u> (John 1:30).

The inconsistencies in your teachings are abundant. Consistent with traditional Christian belief, how could we have failed to properly understand the scriptures when both the Apostle John and Paul wrote in the account of John the Baptist, (John 1:15) "Qui post me venturus est, quia prior me erat" *(He who will come later, was before me)?*

These scriptures are not talking about time, but rather the position or honor of Jesus, and that is, why from the other evangelists, we read "greater than" (Math. 3:11, Mark 1:7, Luke 3:16). *John the Baptist was simply saying that Christ was the author and he (John) was dependent. Historically, John the Baptist was first, but he was preparing the way for the mission of Jesus Christ.* Even if we look carefully at the words in John, the belief in the human nature of Christ is supported. In John 1:27, we read, "Hic est de quo dixi, post me venit vir, qui ante, &c." (this is the one of whom I spoke when I said: after me a <u>man</u> will come who is before me &c.).

But John calls Jesus the "word" and says the "word" was made flesh (John 1:14). *How could the "word" be human in nature and then be made flesh?*

The confusion here is partly because the Greek word ΕΥΕΥΕΤΟ (there was) was translated as "was made." It should have simply been translated as "he was," so the meaning should have been "the word was flesh." In fact, the same Greek word ΕΥΕΥΕΤΟ is translated in John 1:14 as simply "he was." In the Greek, the nouns, *beginning* or *origin,* are indicated by the same Greek noun αρχη (authority). The use of this Greek noun does not always indicate the primal creation, as we can see in many scriptures (John 6:64, 15:17, Acts 11:15, 2Thess. 2:13, 1 John 2:7, 8 &11, 2 John 5&6). For these passages to be understood, we need to pay attention to the context of what is being said.

Exactly! And that is why you are in error, because a contextual understanding of "word" in John 1:14 supports the understanding that *Jesus was present and eternal at the primal creation.*

Haven't we already gone over all of this?

Yes, but I am far from satisfied with your answers! The gospel is about the atonement of the eternal Jesus Christ for our sins. Do you see the meaning of the gospel as different from this?

Commonly "The Gospel" has come to mean the historical writings of the life of Jesus. In truth, "the gospel" means: God's message of the remission of sins, and the gift of eternal life. It is the subject matter of all of the evangelists. When we read in the New Testament, "In the beginning," we should always take that to mean the beginning of the "gospel" (Phil. 4:15).

So what you are saying is that the "word," as it is used in John 1:14 refers to the *beginning of the gospel, and not to the eternal Jesus Christ and the beginning of primal creation?*

Yes, of course!

Since you have gone against what is commonly believed in Christianity, when do you say this beginning was?

The gospel began when John the Baptist, began to preach. It was then that we began to hear the good news of the atonement into the remission of sins by universal baptism. *With the preaching of John the Baptist we gained the hope of the gospel promise (Mark 1&c.). Another way to say this is that the gospel began with an understanding of the quest for salvation.*

Don't we get mixed up here? We say that *"in the beginning was the word",* and at the same time were saying that this *"beginning" was when John the Baptist began to preach?*

Yes, in a way we do, so let me try to clear things up. We have, in a sense, two beginnings here; *first the timeframe for the inception of the gospel, and second the authorship of the gospel. In linear time, the gospel began with the preaching of John the Baptist, but the author of the gospel always remains Jesus Christ.* John the Baptist was sent to prepare the way for Jesus (Malachi 3:1, Mark 1:2). In the beginning of the gospel (prelude), John the Baptist was addressing the Jewish people. The preaching of John the Baptist brought many people to Christ. *John the Evangelist taught without reservation that Jesus Christ was the author of salvation and John the Baptist was sent to prepare the way (John 1:6 &c).*

How can you possibly believe this? **The traditional Christian belief of our time is superior because the scripture clearly states, "In the beginning, the word was <u>with God</u>," i.e., <u>not</u> John the Baptist.**

"With God" was added because John wanted to make two things clear; first, the origin of the gospel was with God (not humans), secondly, because of the fact that Jesus Christ was not personally present when John the Baptist began to preach; it was only appropriate to refer to Jesus and his mission as the "word."

PRIESTHOOD

Now I understand what you believe concerning the human nature of Jesus Christ, and the way he was made divine and the absolute king of the people of God (the author of our salvation), through his obedience to the will of God. I also understand how you believe Jesus to be the individual and only begotten son of God, i.e., united with God. **What I don't understand from what you have said is: how is Jesus our high priest in eternity?** *Certainly, here you will not go against common beliefs that the priesthood applies to the duty of Jesus Christ as it is united with the name Christ (Psalms 110:4, Hebrews 6:20), and the Will of God, or God's word!*

You are right! **Not only because of the implications of the name Christ, but also in the significance of the anointing of prophets before the name Christ was used (Exodus 29:7 & I Kings 19:16).**

60

If this is the case, how do you connect the anointing of prophets *to the priesthood of Christ?*

Do you deny that Jesus was "anointed by God" (Acts 10:38)? *From God himself, Jesus is to be called the "anointed king of the people of God."*

So how do you divide what is of the king, and what is of the high priest? Couldn't we just say, from what you have taught, *Christ is the king, i.e., priesthood is within his duties as king?*

No. *We need to understand that the priesthood of Jesus Christ is his perpetual duty and concern to atone for our sins.*

If I was having trouble with your beliefs before, it is nothing compared to the trouble I am having now! Didn't Jesus pay for our sins on the cross? Wasn't this done before he ascended into heaven to sit on the right hand of God (Hebrews 1:3)? Are you saying that there is something else to understand than Jesus atoned for our sins through his blood and sacrifice on the cross (Hebrews 10:14 & Revelations 1:5)?

Yes, I am. I agree the scriptures that you quoted would lead to the conclusions that have been drawn by many (as you yourself have), however we should look at passages that will give us a fuller understanding of the *atonement.*

I'm incredulous, but please go on.

First, let's look at the title of high priest. A high priest is one who offers sacrifice to atone for sin (Hebrews 5:1). *The duty of a high priest does not come and go. Christ holds that duty perpetually. So that Jesus Christ would be able to be faithful and merciful in his duty as high priest, he was made "similar in all things to his brothers."*

So, how do you define *"similar in all things to his brothers"*?

He would experience all the pain, suffering, disappointment, and even cruel death that humans can experience.   And, it was through these experiences that we as humans are atoned to Christ, i.e., those who through obedience can expect the gift of salvation (eternal life). So it is written, "in eo enim in quo passus est ipse et tentatus, potest iis qui tentantur auxiliary" (in the experience and suffering that he has endured, he of his self is able to offer succor to those who have been tempted) Hebrews 2:18. These words indicate a perpetual care and defense that only Jesus can give his own in order to free them from sin.

So if this atonement is a perpetual thing, why has it been referred to in the holy word in the perfect tense, i.e., "atonement now made"?

The reality that Jesus shed his blood, and by obedience has obtained his duty as high priest should be described as past perfect in time.

You talk about Jesus' death on the cross, and the shedding of his blood, but you fail to mention this as an offering. If the death on the cross was not Jesus offering himself for us, how can we possibly make sense of the offering that Jesus would make for us?

I understand your frustration here! I am fully aware of the common beliefs on atonement, and I realize that what I am about to say will be both unusual and new; however, I firmly believe it to be correct, so I will explain. The idea of an offering should be connected with Christ's duty to atone for our sins. The offering of atonement did not take place on the cross through the shedding of the blood of Christ as is commonly believed. The offering by Jesus Christ for our sins took place in heaven after the resurrection. It was done by Jesus Christ personally before God. That is why the comparison is made between Jesus Christ and the high priest Aaron in Hebrews 9:24 & Hebrews 9:7 & Leviticus 16:12; however, on the other hand, the public shedding of the blood of the sacrificial lamb can be compared with the death of Jesus Christ on the cross.

In my mind this raises two monumental questions. First, of what sort was the *personal offering* that Jesus Christ made in heaven before God the father? Secondly, if Jesus himself was not the *offering,* how do we connect the atonement for our sins to some sort of *abstract offering in heaven?*

We can connect Jesus to the atonement of our sins because the Apostle Paul testified to it as I explained earlier.

For my part, you have just left my question unanswered!

The offering that remains in heaven is not a tangible sacrifice, it is the perpetual love that Jesus has for his followers. It is the reality of the love of Jesus Christ that we must place our faith.

Now this whole explanation seems even <u>*less*</u> *probable; it is to the point now where I am having trouble understanding what you are saying. Please, if I am to grasp what you are saying, can you tell me more of your* unusual beliefs *on the subject of* atonement?

Atonement is the liberation from our sins by Jesus Christ.

A REFUTATION OF COMMON BELIEFS CONCERNING THE JUSTIFICATION OF JESUS CHRIST FOR OUR SINS

In order for our sins to be forgiven, *divine justice* must be satisfied. *How is this possible in heaven? Wasn't it through Christ's death on the cross that reparation for our sins was made?*

The liberation from sin does not come from justification. Justification and liberation are in fact at odds one with another. It is by the power of Jesus Christ that we are forgiven our sins (Philippians 3:23). By the power of Jesus Christ, we are freed from death (the greatest penalty of sin) (Romans 6:23). *God gave Jesus the power to forgive sin, and that is all there is in justification (Romans 3:22, Ephesians 4:32-34).*

In a way, what you are saying is that divine justice is irrelevant! For Devine justice to be relevant, our sins must be punished, i.e., there must be reparation in order for us to be granted forgiveness! How is forgiveness possible without physical reparation?

What you are talking about is our human justice, or crime and punishment. We must put God on a higher plane. If we think God is vengeful, we are undermining the goodness and mercy of God. Divine justice has nothing to do with what we commonly call "the work of man" or "an accomplishment," because through Jesus Christ, God's gift of forgiveness is free!

Why do you say *"that the forgiveness of sin cannot be called an accomplishment"?*

Accomplishments are of our human reality, and the reality of God is entirely different. Let's think about this. If one sins and should be punished, but yet one avoids the punishment because they are forgiven, are they not yet guilty of committing that original sin?

64

You have a point there but don't we carry our sins, and have the ability to transfer sin in the same way money is transferred, and thereby be forgiven?

By no means! Money which represents the common wealth can be exchanged freely. Sin is a personal violation of the laws of God that perpetually adhere to the violator. God forbade the transference of sins (Deut. 24:16, 2 Kings 14:16, Ezekiel 18:24). And let's look at this in a different way. Death is the punishment of sin. Can we transfer our mortality back and forth? It is only by thinking beyond our accustomed reality that we can understand the concept of divine justification.

Okay. If we separate our accustomed reality of crime and punishment, or barter and trade, from the idea of justification of sin, then where are we? Do we find God's majesty is derogated by attempts at reparation? Don't we find a God that does not care about sin?

No, we find an all powerful God that forgives sin completely from his goodness. Can you forgive someone without demanding reparation? If God could not do this and more, he would be less powerful than we as humans are.

Then if God directly and liberally forgives sin without any need of reparation, what is the work of atonement, or how is the anger of God placated? Or to put this more bluntly, is the life and death of Jesus Christ on the cross even relevant to salvation?

I can understand your angst, so I will explain. The anger of God is perpetual; he punishes those who break his laws. Reparation and placation are two different things. God, because of his omnipotence and divine goodness, does not require reparation for sin from us or Jesus Christ! Placation, or what we commonly call the "peace of Jesus Christ," has been given to us as a gift from God through Jesus Christ.

If the *origin of "peace with God"* is not with Jesus Christ, why in the scriptures is it described as *"in Christ"*?

There are three reasons for this. First, Jesus fought against sin, and through his own faultless obedience to God, gained the victory over the penalties of sin. Secondly, through his victory over sin by which he gained eternal life, he obtained for us the right to share in his kingdom, i.e., to be forgiven for our sins. And finally, he laid out the path to follow to reach him. When we are united with Jesus, we are at one in peace with God, and that is what is meant by atonement "in Christ."

It is subtly put, but is what you are saying, *"The origin of peace with God is not in Christ"*?

Yes, basically, that is what I am saying. You will not find one single place in the scriptures where "peace with God" is said to originate with Jesus Christ! We read in the scriptures things like: "Because God loved us, he sent Jesus to the world" (I John 4:10), "Christ visited us in the tender mercy of God" (Luke 4:78). In many places in the holy word we see that God desired peace with mankind prior to the life of Jesus Christ. God's work of atonement actually started with baptism for the remission of sins and the preaching of John the Baptist, and historically, this was prior to the mission of Jesus Christ. Jesus himself, in Luke 4:21, described his mission as "a confirmation of placation, or peace with God." From the prophecies of Isaiah, Chapter 61, it is clear that Jesus would come to "return the captives to God," not to placate God. In Mark 1:14 and in Luke 4:43, Jesus is described as one sent from God who would preach repentance for the remission of sins. Repentance was preached from the beginning of the mission of Jesus (Math.4:17 & Mark 1:15).

So if reconciliation is by God and with God, why did the Apostle Paul so often say that reconciliation with God was made <u>*through*</u> *Jesus Christ?*

It is that God, separate from Jesus, reconciles us to himself <u>through</u> Jesus (2 Cor.5:18). *You won't read anywhere in the holy word that Christ by himself reconciles us to God! Jesus Christ leads us from our errors to God (Romans 5:10).*

I'm glad you mentioned Romans 5:10 because there it clearly states: *"We are reconciled to God through the death of his son." How can you get anything else from this, than that Jesus atoned for our sins by his death on the cross?*

There is nowhere in the Bible that it says that by the death on the cross, Jesus atones for our sins! The meaning of this scripture is that we are brought to God, not God to us; i.e., from the grammatical usage we can see that the motion is toward God. We can see here that it is from the charity of God that we are saved, and a part of that charity was that God allowed Jesus to die on the cross. How can the death on the cross be seen as an appeasement of an angry God? God is a God of love, not anger. Should we really see all of this as an angry God demanding the blood of his son to placate his own Anger? This would be inwardly very inconsistent!

Okay then, you must have some other way of explaining why the Apostle Paul believed we are reconciled to God through the death of Jesus Christ?

Yes, I do. *God permitted his Son to die because the wrongful death of Jesus Christ on the cross was an act that would bind his follower to him. By being bound to Jesus, we become participants in God's eternal favor. Hideous death is the specter that haunts us all. Death is the ultimate wage of sin. For Jesus to lead us through this specter, to blessed eternal life with God, (Hebr. 5:8 &c, Hebr.9:12), he had to pass through the same portal of death as the rest of us and overcome death through resurrection (Hebr.2:14-15, Deut.21:23, Gal. 3:l5). So what I am trying to say here is that for us to follow Jesus to eternal life, we need to relate to him as one of us (I Peter 3:18)!*

I do not doubt your sincerity, *but why would the Apostle Paul call Jesus Christ our mediator with God, (I Timothy 2:5) il, in fact, he does not mediate with God to bring reconciliation?*

The common belief that mediation equals reconciliation is wrong. I will admit that in a way, Jesus does reconcile us to God, *but the initiation of reconciliation should always be seen as of God alone.*

Then, what do you believe is meant by Jesus being our mediator?

Mediator, when it is used properly in the holy word has two meanings: *messenger* and *interpreter. So the proper meaning in these places is that Jesus was a messenger from God who would interpret God's will (Gal. 3:10 & 20).*

How is Jesus a mediator in heaven?

The Latin root of mediator is "medio" or middle, and in reality, Jesus is between God and humans because *everything that God wills for humanity goes through Jesus, and whenever humans seek God they must do it through Jesus (I Cor. 8:6 & Hebr. 7:25). The common way this is understood is that Jesus mediates for us in heaven; however the mediation spoken of in the Bible refers to the time Jesus was on the earth.* For this reason, the Apostle Paul compared Jesus to Moses (Hebr. 8:5&c & Gal. 3:19). *Properly what should be understood here is that Jesus was a mediator that led the people from the "old law of Moses" to the "new covenant with God" (John 1:17, Hebr.7:19, Hebr. 10:1, 2Cor. 3:13, Hebr. 8:9&13, 2Cor.3:14,).* Jesus was a messenger from God who would become the absolute king of his people (John 1:18, 2 Cor. 3:14&16&c, Colos.2:9, 2 Cor. 4:4, John 14:9, Hebr.1:3, Hebr. 9:15 &12:24, Hebr.13:20, Rev14:6, Dan. 9:27, Mark 14:14, Mark13:14).

And yet, what did Paul mean when he said, "God put forth Jesus as a placation" (Romans 3:25)?

Nothing other than Jesus shows us the way to peace with God as it says in Romans 3:25, "God put forth *placation,* through *faith* in the blood of Christ."

From this scriptural reference, it seems rather obvious that placation is in "the blood of Christ." How can you see this any other way?

The meaning of "in the blood of Christ" could have as easily been "on the blood of Christ," because in Latin, preposition usage can be somewhat optional, and this can lead to a multitude of misunderstandings. The same sort of usage can be found in Luke 22:20 & Hebr. 13:20. Often when "the blood of Christ" is mentioned, it is joined with "faith," so the whole meaning is "faith in the blood of Christ." *The blood of Christ is mentioned here because the shedding of Christ's blood completed the earthly mission of Jesus, and with that completion, we have the potential of eternal life with Christ.*

WHY JESUS CHRIST HAD TO DIE

If we are not brought to God by the blood of Christ, and justification is from God alone, *why did Jesus have to die the way he did? Doesn't it seem rather cold that God would not spare his own son such a horrible death?*

In the question, I see the two horns of the double-horned dilemma. I do not want to be gored by either one! Let me just say the cruel death of Jesus Christ should instill in us a love of God, and be remembered as a symbol of our liberation from the penalties of sin. *Even if there was no other reason for Christ to die such a violent death, the reason would be that many of his followers would die of violent and cruel deaths.*

How does this make any sense? If salvation was dependent on God alone, the horrible death of Jesus and his followers seems avoidable? Why didn't God save them all?

<u>God does not change the general nature of things</u>! There may be exceptions to this because God has it in his power to affect changes in nature, *but they are very rare and very specific. God could not have made such changes without changing the general course of nature.*

How can you explain the *general course of nature* so that it would justify those innocent deaths?

What deters murder is our natural tendency to fight a murderer, or to seek revenge. Jesus and the martyrs were full of love, and refused to fight or seek revenge. Because it was so easy to kill these people without apparent consequences, it became an incentive for more *murder*.

Your argument is that God will not change the general course of *nature;* and that can be seen to explain the death of the martyrs. *However, you have said Jesus did not die on the cross for our sins, and God can make a specific change in the general nature of things, why didn't God make an exception for our savior Jesus Christ?*

Because Jesus Christ is the savior of his followers, he had to be an example of obedience even unto death. *If Jesus is to aid those oppressed by sin, he had to understand their suffering, and they had to be able to see that their master suffered even more that they did.* How could Jesus liberate his follower through his example from all evil unless he suffered even more than they did?

I follow your logic here. Are there scriptures to back up your *novel beliefs?*

Yes, and they are as clear in their meaning! In the first part of the letter written by the Apostle Peter, Chapter 2 & 4, and the last part of the letter of Paul in Hebrews 2 & 4, *the message is clear that the reason for the suffering of Christ was, so he could aid those suffering from sin because he had experienced all of their same suffering.*

THE INTERCESSION OF JESUS CHRIST FOR OUR SINS

If common beliefs are in error, how does Jesus *intercede* for us, and how is his intercession related to the *priesthood?*

As it is written in the Holy Bible; the duty of the priesthood of Christ is *intercession* (Hebrews 7:25).

How is intercession unitary with the power of Christ if it does not originate from Christ? How can Christ carry our sins to God if they cannot be borne?

The answer is that he is our eternal high priest with the power given from God to forgive sins, and thus he unites us with God; he does not need to bear our sins. Jesus Christ has the power given from God to succor us. If Jesus of himself held this power, how could we separate Jesus from the one and only God!

Then why are God and Jesus always spoken of as united in the priesthood?

THE DIVINE POWER OF JESUS CHRIST

They are not always spoken of as united.   In John 5:22 & 23 Jesus and God are referred to separately: *"The father was not to judge, but gave judging to the son, so that all who honor the son, thus honor the father."*[14] It is clear here that Jesus is, by himself, the ultimate judge by God-given power.

Your tenacity amazes me; how, when it suits you, you can draw great generalizations! This quotation is only talking about the office of judge that Jesus will have on the final day! How can it be seen to separate the father from the son?

Nobody would deny that in Hebrew, the word *"judge"* is associated with power (control, governance, direction, guidance etc.). Thus the highest judge is always God himself (Psalms 2:10 and Genesis 18:25)! All honor, goes to God, who through Jesus, has offered salvation by establishing Christ's kingdom. This, however, *does not make them united in person.*

If you cannot show me more compelling scriptural evidence that supports your belief, isn't this statement without verity?

There are many scriptures that declare Jesus to be absolute in power!

How am I to believe that Jesus is king right now? *It seems very probable to me that his kingdom is of the future, and heaven is ruled by the Father, Son and Holy Ghost!*

The scriptures testify that <u>now</u> Jesus Christ sits on the right hand of God (Revelations 3:21 and Romans 8:24). To be seated on the right hand of God means that Jesus was given the *honor and power* to *rule his kingdom,* and now he is the sole *merciful judge of his people.*

It is well understood that Jesus sits at the right hand of God in glory; *why do you emphasize honor?*

One comes to the emphasis of honor placed upon Jesus, by thinking through the meaning of what the Apostle Paul said: at that time Jesus is not subjected to God, but rules in the place of God (I Cor. 15:24 & 28). *Christ was given the honor by God to be the absolute ruler and judge of the people of God. In his place of honor he is our high priest, and holds the Divine power within us (Math. 28:18, Ephes. 1:22 & c, Rev. 5:12).*

It seems that you are grasping at straws here, so you can avoid the more important ideas represented by the image of Jesus sitting on the "right hand of God,". Do you accept the Biblical translations of Erasmus* and Vatablus?*

Yes, I have a great deal of respect for Erasmus and Vatablus.

Let me quote from the translation of Erasmus for part of 1st Hebrews: "Portansaqua omnia verbo virtutis suae" (upholding all by his own virtuous word). *This quotation demonstrates; the power of the words of Christ within his church; it in no way shows that he is separate from God.* Without further scriptural evidence, I find your attempts to separate the power of Jesus and God *weak, at best.*

(*Desiderius Erasmus Roterodamus, Dutch Renaissance humanist, scholar, teacher, and Catholic priest born October 28, 1466 died July 12, 1536)

(*Francis Vatablus of Gastled: French Hebrew scholar, Born early 16th century, died March 16, 1547)

I have further scriptural evidence to support the individuality of the power of Christ. They are all of the scriptures that speak of the power of the Holy Spirit as apart from Jesus. Further, *how do we understand the purpose of Jesus praying to his father in heaven, if his power was not separate from his father?*

Again, you step on your own foot! *In the holy word where we see Jesus praying to the father for us, don't we see the way we too, are to pray to God through Jesus? Or, why, if Jesus is absolute in power does he set an example for us by praying to his father in Heaven?*

Again, the example you cite is from a time when Jesus was to come into his kingdom; i.e., he was living his mortal life on earth. When Jesus lived his mortal life on earth, he preached "the father always heard him" (John 11:42). Another example of the manner in which the life of Jesus can be seen historically is the biblical story of Martha. Before Jesus came into his glory and possession of absolute power, Martha knew that whatever Jesus asked of his father would be granted (John 11:22). *Further, at the time of the earthly life of Jesus, it would have been idolatry for the faithful not to divide the power ascribed to the Holy Spirit from Jesus Christ!*

THE INVOCATION AND ADORATION OF JESUS CHRIST

How can a belief in the harmony of the power of God, the Holy Spirit, and Jesus Christ be seen as idolatry?

At the time of the earthly life of Jesus, to ascribe the power of the Holy Spirit or God to Jesus would have substituted Jesus in the place of God; i.e., he would have become an idol!

Then, why did Jesus say over and over again, "whatever you ask in my name shall be granted unto you" (John 14:13 & 14)? And we read a similar promise in John 15:16 & 16:23, assuring us that Jesus could accomplish the things sought of God. How else can you see the secret or open intercession for us as anything other than Jesus intercedes for us, past present and future?

Don't you get a little confused in your understanding of these passages if Jesus was already a god while he lived on earth, and at the same time, he is interceding and praying to God for us? Further, doesn't this confused view of Jesus make it impossible for us to understand and relate to him?

I can understand and relate to him better this way! Can you show me further proof in the scriptures to support your beliefs?

I could do that, but what better way to correct you than to use the same scriptures that you have already cited! *When Jesus says "he intercedes for us," he is saying in effect that he is* separate from us and God; i.e., as an individual he is petitioning the divinity and ultimate power of God. When Jesus is called our eternal high priest, we admit he is subordinate to God by an understanding of the meaning of the word "priest."

If, when Jesus walked the earth, he believed God alone was divine, why would he ask his followers to pray in his name? Why couldn't they just pray to God directly?

Jesus instructed his disciples to pray in his name in order to acknowledging him as their high priest, and as a method of supporting them in the future. Jesus was made high priest not from his own deity, but from the divinity of God the Father (Hebrews 5:5).

Alright, I have to admit that there can be problems with seeing Jesus as continually praying for us in heaven. *How do you believe that Jesus intercedes for us?*

Let me just say, the idea that Jesus carries our sin to God is false. Trinitarian beliefs rely on the idea that sin can be carried or transferred. *When we say that Christ intercedes for us, we are saying that the obedient life of Jesus gives us the possibility of unity with God. Today when we talk about praying in the name of Jesus Christ, the meaning should be "praying to Jesus Christ."*

Your beliefs fly in the face of the teachings of the Apostle Paul. Paul clearly teaches that we do not petition Jesus directly! You rely too heavily of your speculations. Where are your beliefs actually supported in scripture?

God's power rests in Jesus. That the one and only God is the ultimate power in heaven can be clearly seen in the Old Testament; when God was evoked, it was said, "by the power of

God" (Gen.12:8, Exod. 34:5, Joel 2:32). God and Jesus became one in purpose. Just as God in the Old Testament was evoked with the words, "by the power of God," today God may be evoked "by his power that is in Jesus," or Jesus alone (John 15:16 & 16:23). So when we pray to Jesus, we are praying to God, and if we join the ancient Latin and Syrian versions of John 14:14, we read, "Si quid petieritis me in nomine meo, hoc faciam," *(whatever you ask me in my name, you shall be granted).*

The way you have interpreted the ancient texts has to be wrong! Paul clearly stated: "We pray to the Father in the name of the Son," if we only need address Jesus in our prayers, why don't we just address Jesus and leave out "in the name of Jesus Christ"?

Because the Syrian and Ancient Latin translations I just used (John 14:14) are not found in the Greek, *you might be correct,* but even if we remove the "of me" so that it is written simply "whatever you ask in my name," your beliefs are at odds with scriptural truth. Let's discuss what is contained in the meaning of the words *"in my name."* To ask in the *name* of someone or something is to evoke the power of the mentioned, as we see often in the New Testament (John 17:11 & 12, Ephes. 1:21, Hebr. 1:4). So, when we say in the "name of Jesus Christ," we are simply saying "by the power of Jesus Christ." We can see the same thing in the Old Testament in Psalms, "In the name of Jehovah, I will destroy them", i.e., by the power of Jehovah they will be destroyed (Psalms 18:10-12, & 46:6, etc.). It would have been correct, if it would have been said of Jesus: *"Whatever you ask of Jesus Christ will be done by his power."* So you can see that however John 14:14 is interpreted, the meaning is the same! *Jesus wanted his disciple to understand they were to address him directly while acknowledging his power was God-given.*

In a way, haven't you removed God the Father from the picture?

No! Jesus was instructing his disciples about the change that would occur with the completion of his mission. He was assuring the disciples that in the *future,* **they could seek him, as they had sought his father in the past; i.e.,** *he would have sufficient power from the Father to answer their prayers.*

I can see that whatever I present as normal and plain in understanding of belief, you will have some other view. **Even though your arguments seem to have a consistency to them, what bothers me,** *is your contrary attitude. I am forced by conviction to match it. The disciples were commanded by Jesus to "Pray to the Father in his name", period! From the time of Jesus and the disciples, and throughout the history of Christ's holy church the teaching on this has been the same: we follow the commandment to pray to God in the name of Jesus Christ!* **How can anything be clearer than this?**

I don't agree that the disciples were, in fact, commanded; they were encouraged or advised to pray in that manner.

Then why did the Apostle Paul command that everything was to be done in the name of the Lord Jesus (Colossians 3:17)?

I guess what I object to here, is the emphasis on form. What is more important is to understand that where the Lord Jesus is mentioned by the Apostle Paul, Paul is making reference to the teachings of Jesus Christ, and that we move forward within those teachings. That is why Jesus, at the end of his earthly mission, instructed his disciples (John 16:25), "Now the time comes when

I do not speak to you in proverbs, but I will openly show you the Father." This scripture clearly illustrates the change that would occur in the future, when the disciples would live in the "word" of the Lord Jesus.

Can you understand how the vast majority of Christians would take these words of Jesus to mean *in the future, Jesus would be able to intercede for them because of his favor with God?*

Yes, I can! And, in fact, I can see how the common understanding is simpler, more direct, and fits! I can also see how the common interpretation would fit and be supported by scriptures in the Old Testament. Isn't all of this convention, though? If Jesus is seen as an agent here, perpetual work is implied. If Jesus wanted his disciples to understand a perpetual work in heaven, he would have explained it. There is no mention in the scriptures of ongoing heavenly work for Jesus. Jesus simply wanted his disciples to understand that they could pray to him in the future as they had prayed to God in the past.

Then it seems strange that Jesus would say, (John 16:26-27 "et no dico vobis, quod ego rogaturus sim Patrem pro vobis, ipse enim Pater amat vos & c." *(I won't talk to you, so that I can petition the Father for you, in the Father you are loved). How is it possible that what you have said is consistent with this statement by Jesus?*

Jesus certainly did not want us to understand that he had some further work to do, as I explained earlier! Jesus was using poetic language here. With this poetic use of language, Jesus was emphasizing the primacy of God the Father! There is hidden meaning here. *The primary idea of this poetic use of language is the time sequence; i.e., the present time compared to the future.*

Jesus was saying that in the future, the disciples could petition him as the father. If I may, let me turn this poetry into prose: "My work is now complete; through my examples and teachings, I have shown you the will of the Father. With the perfection of my work, I have been given absolute power in heaven from our completely good God of love. Take faith and have no fear, for I will now enable you in your work by answering your prayers and letting you see the truth in all things. Always remember the source of good and love is God the Father".

In your prose example, you mention "work" three times. Why would the intentions of Jesus in this statement been so involved with "work" if, as you say, "Jesus has no future work to do with God?

The earthly work of Christ goes on (John 17:4). The sense of this passage is that when Jesus was gone, those involved in his "work" would be able to seek him through faith and prayer, and would have the Holy Spirit to strengthen them internally.

I am glad we have spent so much time on the passages in John (John 14:14 & 15:16 &16:23). *You have explained yourself well, and in a way, I do not have a problem with addressing Jesus Christ directly in prayer. My problem is that most of your belief rests on reason. I must ask you if you can support your beliefs by adhering more strictly to the Holy Bible.*

Please allow me to thank you, because your questions have allowed me to explain and defend my understanding of Christian religion. And now so that you have no doubt about what it means to pray in the name of Christ, from the gospel of John we read: (John 16:24), "Usque modo non petiistis quidquam in nomine meo: Petite et accipietis" (up until now you have not been able to ask anything in my name: now you can). There are two important concepts to glean from this scripture: first, before this time Jesus had used Divine power to answer calls for help in person, i.e., in Luke 17:5 and Math. 8:25 where we read how Jesus calmed the storm; secondly, after the separation of Jesus from his disciples, they could no longer address him in person, so they were to ask him *"in his name."*

Maybe I have missed something here, but it seems that you have just *undermined* *everything you have said about the human nature of Christ. You have said "that Jesus (of only human nature) received his divinity and absolute power in heaven after death." How is the human Jesus using his* *own divine power* *to perform miracles?*

We cannot understand any of this without a sense of *historical time sequence.* When Jesus spoke these words, he had not yet departed to the Father; he was talking about a time soon to come, when he would be in heaven; i.e., we read just before John 16:24 (in John 14:12), "I say to you, he that believes in my work will perform even greater works than I, because I go to the Father, and whatever is asked in my name, I will do, so that the Father will be glorified in the son." *Can anyone have trouble seeing that Jesus is talking about the future here!* It should be clear that the disciples could pray to Christ in the future, and that fact has little to do with them praying to him while he was on the earth.

Okay. let's talk about *time sequence then!* If the divine power of Jesus was not his own, *how do you explain the divine power of Jesus as it relates to the time when Jesus walked the earth, or how are we to understand miracles that Jesus performed during the time of his life on earth?*

When Jesus prayed in order to raise Lazareth from the dead, he said (John 11:42), "Pater gratias ago tibi, quoniam audisti me. Ego autem sciebam, quod simper me audis; sed propter populu qui cirumstat, dixi, ut credent, quod tu me misisti" (Thank you, Father, because you hear me, however you always hear me, but I spoke so that the crowd would believe that you sent me). *We can see from this example, that Jesus was* _endowed_ *with divine power from the beginning of his work on Earth.* That he was able to use this power _independently_ can be seen by the fact that he passed his power to his disciples (Math 10:8). *The way the miracles were performed by Jesus, and the way that Jesus passed his divine power to the apostles, illustrates that he was in individual control of that power. Always though, Jesus made it clear in his prayers that the divine power* _originated from God the Father (John 5:21)._ *The sense of all of this is that Jesus, of human nature, was using his God-given power to do the will of his Father in Heaven (John 10:25).*

Going over what you have said in my mind, I can see how one could find a certain consistency in your beliefs; however I find something _very troubling in all of this._ *If, as you have taught, we believe "the Jesus that walked the earth, and lived a life of obedience to God was ONLY HUMAN IN NATURE, i.e., held nature inherited from humanity, yet within his human nature, he held DIVINE POWER, i.e., nature inherited from divinity, don't we have* _two natures here?_

A REFUTATION OF BELIEF IN JESUS CHRIST

HAVING ADDITIONAL DIVINE OR HUMAN NATURES

I believe if you had paid sufficient attention to my previous answers, you wouldn't be troubled by this question. Your confusion is common and lamentable! The Trinitarians believe that while Jesus Christ is divine in nature, he was also fully human. What could be more inconsistent than believing that Jesus is God, and yet at the same space in time, he was the Son of God? So, in order to remove all doubt, I must prove two things to you: first, that Jesus is only human in nature and does not have an additional nature; secondly, that Jesus was given the divine power from God, who alone has a divine nature.

Can you please spare me your *logic and reason*, and support what you say from the *scriptures?*

I can support our beliefs by what is in the scripture, *and what is* lacking in the scripture! *First, let me say there is no support in scripture for the belief that Jesus has more than one nature. If we want to prove that he did not see himself equal to God, there are many scriptures we can cite.* In Mark 13:32, it clearly states "the Son (Jesus) does not know the day or hour of his coming in glory." Of course, this day and hour would be known to God! In John 14:27 & 28, Jesus denies he is equal to the Father. There are many places in the New Testament where Jesus refers "All glory and honor to the Father". *Trinitarians always say these passages are to be understood figuratively.*

If there is nothing more to the nature of Jesus than, as a human of human nature, he began his life in the womb of the virgin, why did Jesus himself say in John 13:13, "the Son of Man descended from heaven," and repeated in John 6:62, "that he would ascend to the place he had been previously"?

There have been questions raised about the Greek translations of John 3:13 by Erasmus and Beza*. The translation of the second citation is well accepted. These passages are used commonly to support Trinitarian beliefs. *The Trinitarians will alternately say that Jesus as God descended from heaven to become mortal, or that he was both in heaven and on earth.*

(*Theodore Beza (born June 24, 1519 died October 13, 1605) French Protestant theologian and scholar)

There is more support for these beliefs in the holy word than your contentions, for if we go along with your beliefs, how could the Human Christ have been in Heaven before he was resurrected?

The first thing we should ask ourselves is if the scripture indicates that Jesus was in heaven prior to resurrection, does this mean that he had an extra divine nature?

THE ASCENSION AND TIME SPENT IN HEAVEN OF THE

HUMAN CHRIST PRIOR TO HIS MISSION ON EARTH

Even if John 3:13: ("no one has gone up to heaven except the one who has come down from heaven, the Son of Man") is not taken as proof that Jesus is divine in nature, doesn't it clearly show that Jesus lived before he was born to the Virgin Mary. Because we can clearly see from John 6:62 ("What if you were to see the Son of Man ascending to where he was before")[15], that the divine Jesus Christ was in heaven prior to his life on earth?

If Jesus Christ lived in heaven prior to his earthly existence, then his nature could not have been wholly human. But this is not the case, because over and over again, Jesus calls himself the "Son of Man,": i.e., human, and in no verse does he refer to himself as divine! Just as Moses, Jesus went into Heaven before his mission to be with God and to be instructed by God, and likely as not, this happened more than once. In the Old Testament, the example of the way that Moses was instructed by God twice can serve as a model for how Jesus was taught by God (Exodus 19, 24:18, 31:18, 32:15-16). Moses, was with God for forty days! *Mount Sinai was for Jesus and for Moses a meeting place with God; i.e., Heaven (Deut. 4:36).*

This explanation certainly seems convenient. Even though it is unheard of, it gets you out of a dilemma in explaining the verses that mention Jesus was in heaven prior *to his resurrection. I must ask you though, why didn't the Evangelists, in their narration of the life of Jesus Christ, make any mention of Jesus's visit with God as a human prior to resurrection? Certainly something as monumentally important as that should have been mentioned and explained at least once!*

In the first three gospels, it was not mentioned because, just as when Moses talked to God, Jesus was alone. There is an account of this primary ascension mentioned in the last Gospel of John (John 3:31 & 32). John the Baptist describes the primary ascension, "The one who comes from above is above all. The one who is of the earth is earthly and speaks of earthly things. But the one who comes from Heaven (is above all). He testifies to what he has seen and heard, but no one accepts his testimony."[15] John the Evangelist was not a personal witness to this marvelous event. Therefore, he left us this account to be a matter of faith.

Contradictions just seem to mount if this is to be accepted as truth! If this actually happened, why, I beseech you, did the Apostle Paul, in reference to the time after the resurrection say, "Christ entered the holy place only once, i.e., heaven (Hebrews 9:12 & 24)?

This question is best answered by explaining the meaning of Hebrews 9:12 & 24. *The key here is that it says, "he entered after shedding his blood."* This scripture is comparing the death of Christ and the entering of the holy place to the annual sacrifice performed by the Priest Aaron in the Old Testament. The sense should be: "per proprium sanguine intoivit semel in sancta" (through his own blood he entered once into heaven", i.e., *he only entered once through his own blood.* This reference is talking about something entirely different, and can't be compared to the *primary ascension.*

I know that you believe this explanation should satisfy my doubts, but it does not! You beliefs are inconsistent. You compare the sacrifice of Aaron to Jesus. Aaron made a blood sacrifice to placate and unite the Israelites with God, and yet you say, "that the blood Jesus shed was not a sacrifice to placate God and atone for our sins"?

I compared Jesus to Aaron to say he is human, just as Aaron was human. The shedding of the animal blood was for the benefit of the humans; not to appease an angry God; in the same way, the shedding of the blood of Jesus was relative to his human condition and message.

In Numbers 16:41 & c., Aaron was told by Moses to take lire from the alter, and put in incense to atone for the anger of God. The wrath of God was engendered because they had extinguished the divine lire and murmured against Moses and Aaron. Doesn't this example show us ritual in order to placate an angry God?

This example you cite is different from the annual sacrifice of Aaron. The annual sacrifice of Aaron was not to appease an angry God. It was done to demonstrate obedience to God.

Isn't the Apostle Paul, in Hebrews, talking about the way through Christ we are *justified* to God?

Yes, but not as a work of Christ's priesthood that can be compared to the priestly duties of Aaron. *Nowhere in the scriptures is a priestly <u>work</u> of atonement mentioned for Christ.*

How are we justified, then, by the priestly duties of Jesus Christ?

From the time Jesus sat on the right hand of God, he was given the power to forgive our sins. The gift from God was not bought and paid for; <u>it was free from God's goodness</u>! The priesthood of Jesus began prior to his crucifixion. Christ's priesthood cannot be seen as a justification for sin. What we have inherited from the life of Jesus should be seen as a fulfillment of the decrees of a <u>Perfectly Just and Good God.</u> Even if we look at the special relationship of Jesus with God (which can be supported by reason alone), we need to be careful in ascribing an aspect of "work" to this relationship, for any "work" for Jesus after resurrection is unsupported in the scriptures.

Your answer is about justification, but when we look at the sacrifices of the animals in the Old Testament, wasn't that an offering for sin?

Not at all! Those sheep belonged to God before they were sacrificed. Neither can there be any balance found between an individual offense to God and killing sheep! Even if we were to try to say, sheep for sin, how in the world could one poor animal compensate for the sins of the society for who they were sacrificed?

When we look at the vows of God, and the way he destroyed the disobedient and spared the obedient who sacrificed to him, couldn't these sacrifices be seen as propitiation?

He did not save them because they were paid in full! He saved them of himself!

Why did he save them then?

He saved them in fulfillment of his promises, and out of his divine kindness.

Are you saying that the Death on the cross should be understood in the same way?

Yes! Jesus was obedient in every way, even to the shedding of his blood and death on the cross. The works of Christ (including his death on the cross) were accomplished during his lifetime on earth. God did not will Christ to die so a price would be paid for our sins. Jesus did not come in order to bear our sins. Jesus died on the cross in fulfillment of the promises and decrees of God that have their source in God's divine goodness. God, from his love, gave us Jesus. Jesus Christ our king is now has absolute power, so he can grant us eternal life and well-being, he can liberate us from death, misery and ruin, which are the real penalties of sin.

CONCLUSION

I consider it my good fortune and a privilege that over thirty years ago, I became *curious about the lack of any English language translations of Fausto Sozzini's own work. Further, that my curiosity led me to make an American English translation, and interpretation* of Fausto Sozzini's <u>Very Brief Instruction of Christian Religion</u>. *This project has enriched my understanding of the Christian religion and western world intellectual history, and this effort has given me a greater appreciation of the intellectual freedom that we enjoy in the United States and the intellectual roots of that freedom. It is my hope that this work will help others to understand and appreciate the intellectual work of Fausto Sozzini, and the important place of Sozzini's work in the history of world political and religious opinion.*

One can understand from reading the <u>Very Brief Instruction in Christian Religion,</u> that Fausto Sozzini does <u>not</u> deny the divinity of Jesus Christ. He explains Christ's divinity differently; i.e., *Jesus becomes divine after his resurrection.* <u>Sozzini does not base salvation on reason</u>. *For Sozzini the source of salvation is* the free gift of a purely good god. Sozzini does deny the doctrine of the Trinity, and Arian doctrine because he has only God the Father and Jesus in the godhead, the nature of Jesus is entirely human, and he does not allow for the existence of Jesus Christ before his birth in the womb of the Virgin Mary. One can easily surmise from this dialogue that Fausto Sozzini was not, strictly speaking, reformatory in his theology, like John Calvin or Martin Luther; his theology was revolutionary. His theological explanations of the nature of Jesus Christ and the mystery of the godhead are novel, and in many ways, without precedence. Where Martin Luther and John Calvin wanted to return Christianity to a purer form based on acceptance of the Nicene and Apostles' Creeds, Sozzini rejected the belief in the holy Trinity. He believed that traditional Christian teachings about creeds were extra to Bible scripture and the source of many of the problems within Christianity.

Although we could say that Sozzini was part of the "historical reformation," his theology was separate and revolutionary. Sozzini's theological dialogue may have saved the Unitarian movement and opened doors to the future. His purely human Christ would give a theological foundation to humanism. His theological explanations concerning the relationship of God to nature ("God does not interfere with the normal course of nature") would establish a strong connection between humanistic philosophy and nature, i.e., an independent human nature, with the power and responsibility to affect the general course of nature (for better or for worse), that would strongly influence the work of nature writers to our present day. By elevating the prominence of human deeds and reason over dogma, Sozzini laid a theological foundation for tolerance.

I hope that this translation (and interpretation) has in a small way brought back to life *a very important part of the crucible of religious opinion that existed for a short time in Poland and Transylvania in the sixteenth century, the diversity of religious opinion that would create the need for toleration that would become so fundamental in establishing modern democratic society. I also hope that this translation of the Very Brief Instruction in Christian Religion illustrates how difficult it can be for theologians of good intention to come to agreement of opinion on the profound mysteries of the godhead. And maybe like me, you have grown fond of these two theologians portrayed by Fausto Sozzini in the Very Brief Instruction of Christian Religion; they give us a glimpse (through their classical dialogue) into a time very different from our own when the art of theological language and debate was held in such high esteem.*

In the final analysis, we must find that Fausto Sozzini was a polemicist; his Very Brief Instruction in Christian Religion is in classical dialogue form, and may very well be a historical vignette that captures much of the spirit and substance of the theological debates that were organized to test the opinions of early Unitarian theologians in Poland in the late sixteenth century. One can easily walk away from the Instruction in Christian Religion in agreement with the Sozzinian theology, traditional Christian theology, or some other opinion. And this raises a very important question: Was Sozzini trying to change the matrix of traditional Christian belief, or was he doing something else? The something else (if you will) could be what has been referred to as the mystery of Socinianism. Was Sozzini trying to break down what he viewed as a staid theological dogma in order to change what he perceived as corrupt Christian values? Could he have simply been pointing to the value of continuing research and debate on the mysteries of the godhead? Was he making a case for a less optimistic view of dogma? Was he trying to provide a consistent theological argument to unite the Polish brethren? [14] Was it all of the above and more? For me, and I hope for you, this translation and interpretation will raise many unanswered questions about this brilliant sixteenth century theologian and his time period. More translation, interpretation, and study of the actual work of Fausto Sozzini and others of this fascinating time of religious diversity of opinion are certainly necessary if we are to understand better where our modern world came from theologically, and possibly, how we have erred.

Some things about Sozzini's work are clear. He was not happy with the traditional Christianity of his day. It is clear that he wanted a change in Christian opinion and attitude! He wanted more obedience to the teachings of Jesus. He wanted us to feel positive about our human nature. He put a great deal of importance on our human intellect: "the only part of our specie essence that we share with God." And finally, it is easy to see that Sozzini loved and valued human life and freedom, and simply adored his all powerful king Jesus Christ!

Fausto Sozzini challenges us to study, value language as high art, think, question, to be positive about Christian religion and our human potential (intellect), to be tolerant to those who do not agree with our beliefs and opinions, improve our Christian attitudes ("to be more obedient to the teachings of Jesus"), and to take human responsibility for the "general course of nature"; and the "challenge of Sozzini" may be his greatest contribution to our western intellectual and religious heritage.

Footnotes

---

1. **Pg. 8**   Cory, pp. 63, "There was something noble in this renunciation of a life of refined and pleasant associations. Even a hostile critic admits the "he condemned himself to run through the nations as an unfortunate vagabond"; pp.64, "The following year was blest by the arrival of a little daughter, who was named Agnes after her paternal grandmother."; pp.&74 "When his last call came on March 3rd, Socinus was ready. Though the church was strong and united, he was weary with the strife and controversy, and eager to go to his reward, as he declared to the faithful Stoinski, who was at his side. Socinus' belief in immortality had always been a strong one, and as he drew his last breath, he declared to Stoinski his joy in being released from his labors and obtaining his reward."

2. Pg. 8   Cantu, pp. 490 "Tota lice Baabylon destruxit tect Lutherus Calvinus muros, sed fundamenta Soccinus"

3. Pg. 10   Florida, R. E. "Voltaire and the Socinians"

4. Pg. 10 Allen, Joseph. pp. 122 &123 "But the heresy survived, and took a form more definitely Unitarian. One John Lewes is recorded to have been "burned at Norwich, September 18, 1583, for denying the godhead of Christ." Two years later a clergyman, Francis Ket, was burned at the same place for the same offense. Most of the so-called martyrdoms of Elizabeth's reign may fairly be ascribed to political conspiracies and alarms. The four already recounted would seem to have been the only martyrs of mere opinion. These were concessions to an intolerance more deadly than her own. The Queen, it is evident, had to keep the zeal of her ecclesiastics sharply in hand.

The last example in this kind to be noted is under the reign of James, whose Protestant policy was unhappily dwarfed and warped by his conceit of a "kingcraft" that should purchase terms of amity with the Catholic reaction, then drifting steadily towards the horrors of the Thirty Years' War. At Smithfield, in 1612, Bartholomew Legate---a man "in person comely, complexion black, age about forty years, of a bold spirit, confident carriage, fluent tongue, excellently skilled in the Scriptures"—and at Lichfield, Edward Wightman, were burned at the stake as "Anabaptists and Arianizers." Thus says an historian of the Baptists, "this sect had the honor of leading the way (in 1535) and bringing up the rear of all the martyrs who were burned alive in England." It had been found more expedient, writes Thomas Fuller, that heretics "should silently and privately waste away in prisons, rather than to grace them and amuse others with the solemnity of a public execution."

(Vol.ii, p.64) Pg.124, "As early as 1614, within ten years after the death of Socinus, the "Racovian Catechism," in a Latin version, had been publicly burned in London, and its circulation, so far as might be, had been suppressed. In 1616 the first English church and congregation of independents had been gathered by Henry Jacob, a disciple and companion of John Robinson in Leyden, who afterwards joined the Plymouth colony in America."

5. Pg. 10   The Reverend professor F. J. Foakes Jackson, D.D., from introduction to Faustus Socinus by David M Cory, pg. vii, "A religion based solely on reason cannot be expected to influence the heart, or make its votaries capable of heroic, even if perverse, self sacrifice. It may begin with a fiery repudiation of error, and produce real prophets of scientific thought or poets like Lucretius and Shelley, but it tends inevitably in the end to a frigid indifference to all spiritual interests in their widest sense. If therefore, we place the religion of Laelius and Fausts Socinus in this category, it is small wonder that it fails to have any attraction."

6.   Pg. 11   Cantu`, p.491, Solo il soccianismo impianto` l' autonomia della ragione; e ne derivano Cartisio, Spinosa, Bayle, Hume, Kant, Lessing, Hegel, Bauer, Feuerbach (Only in Socinianism do we find the establishment of autonomy of reason, and from this autonomy of reason are derived the work of Cartesians, Spinoza, Bayle, Hume, Lessing, Hegel, Bauer, and Feuerbach)

7.   Pg. 11   Cory p. 149, "Crypto-Socinianism" had a great vogue in the latter half of the seventeenth and the first half of the eighteenth centuries. Bayle notes the anonymous author of La Politiue du Clerge' de France, whose main point is that the chief danger to French Catholicism did not consist in

the Protestant opposition, but in the Socinians in the church. This author goes on to say, "And what is more terrible is that this is not merely the religion of our young abbots, it is the theology of certain weighty and learned societies and those who make a great parade of the purity of their life and of their attachment for the Catholic faith." The writer evidently had the Port-Royalists in mind, and the famous Antoine Arnauld hastened to publish a denial of the prevalence of such views. That this Socinian strain persisted in the French church is, however, indubitable, and the Eclaircissement of the eighteenth century, while laying a new emphasis upon nature, republished many of the distinctive tenets of Socinianism." Allen, Joseph p. 142-143, "In 1695 appeared Locke's "Reasonableness of Christianity," maintaining that the one "essential" of Christian belief is the acceptance of Jesus as the Messiah. This was at once assailed by John Edwards, son of the author of "Gangraena," with almost all of his father's virulence, charging that Locke was a Socinian but afraid to own it. Locke might well reply, as he did, that he had not read a single Socinian book. But all the charge implied was in the air. Whatever was most free in the heritage of thought, Locke had entered into as deeply as any man."

8.　　　Pg. 19　　　Allen, Joseph pp. 205, "In the year 1832, just while the glow of an earlier controversy was fading out, the first open break was made with the accepted customs of the Congregational order. Ralph Waldo Emerson, minister of the Second Church in Boston (where he had succeeded Henry Ware, Jr., three years before), resigned his charge on the refusal of his church members to discontinue or radically change the order of communion service."

9. Pg. 19   Sargent p. 9, "Galen was placed in the home of a friend from the age of five to seventeen years," an historian explained, "because the family was so large." He saw his parents frequently, however, attended school and church with his brothers and sisters, and revered his family. He was a sickly, quiet boy, loving, devout, and perceptive. Reverend Levi Leonard, pastor of the town's Unitarian church, superintendent of its schools, and founder of its library, the first free public library in America, had a strong, beneficial influence on Galen and his brothers.

10.   Pg. 19 Wolfe pp. 79-80, "It was here, as well as in his classes and in the library of Dr. Butler, that he came under the influence of Agassiz, Wordsworth, Thoreau, and Emerson.

Emerson's name and philosophy were in the very air one breathed at Madison.   Here, as throughout Eastern and Midwestern America, the intellectuals banded into lyceums and literary societies, parroted his wise saying, unconscious for the most part that in the phrases they so glibly mouthed lurked dynamite enough to blast into oblivion their pleasant little worlds of commerce and convention."   pp. 147-148, "In the days that followed, Emerson slipped away alone more than once and came to the mill, where the two of them sat in the hang-nest and talked---the Elijah and Elisha of nature transcendentalism.   The old man listened with Olympian composure, now and then asking a question in "his thrilling voice" to draw Muir out. And so the disciple poured out to his master his long pent up, most intimate thoughts, knowing that in this man who "inhabited eternity," he had at last found perfect understanding.

Without any doubt, Emerson too, found a deep joy in these conversations. For here in the wilderness, doing common labor in a sawmill, he had found the living embodiment of his own Man Thinking, his Poet, who looking upon Nature with unveiled eyes, could integrate the Parts in a mighty whole.

When the Bostonians left the valley, Emerson, loath to part with his friend, asked him to ride with him as far as Clark's Station. Muir, eagerly accepting, suggested they should camp for the night among the Big Trees. Emerson unflanked for the moment by his party, said, "Yes, yes, we will camp out." So Muir counted on at least one good wild memorable night around a sequoia camp-fire." Uninhibited by Thayers, Forbeses, and Hathaways, what talk they might have! And what silences!

The next day as the party made its chattering way through the majestic forest, Muir, keeping close to Emerson, interrupted now and then to call attention to individual trees. Thayer, also riding as near to Emerson as the trail would allow, to take down his every word, became a bit impatient. "We grew learned and were able to tell a sugar pine from a yellow pine, and to name a silver-fir, and the libocedrus . . . second cousin to the Sequoia."

At least once, according to Muir's notes, he succeeded in drawing Emerson aside by quoting a line from his own "Woodnotes", "Come listen to what the pine tree sayeth." It was on a ridge high in a forest where lordly sugar pines dominated. Muir, loving the sugar pine above all other trees, remarked how they spread "their arms with majestic gestures, addressing the surrounding trees like very priests of the woods." Emerson gazed long, and in silence, then said that surely no other forest had "so fine a preacher or so well dressed and well-behaved and devout a congregation."

11.   Pg. 19   Johnston pp. 51, "By the early 1860's, the descriptive writings of James Hutchings, Thomas Starr King and noted *New York Tribune* editor Horace Greeley, had generated national interest in Yosemite."

12.   Pg. 46   The New American Bible (New Testament) Hebrews 1:6, p.339

13.   Pg. 53   Ibid. Ephesians 1:21, pg. 294

14.   Pg. 91   Allen pp. 77, "The confession cited above was published five years before the coming of Fautus Socinus, who did most to organize the movement and has given it a name in history. Its time of chief activity was during and just after the twenty-five years of service he gave it till his death, in 1604; but this service availed only to keep it alive, as a pretty vigorous school of theological opinion, through a period while Protestantism itself was steadily declining in Poland, under the crafty and most iniquitous oppression soon to be described."

15.   Pg. 19   King pp. 26-27 "Mr. Clarke we found a very intelligent man, living alone in the wilderness. To my amazement he knew me. He was born under the shadow of Monadnoc, and has two brothers, I soon learned, who are Unitarian ministers. One of our witty friends in Boston, whenever he has occasion to speak of any man who is worth half a million or so, always says, *sotto voce* and in parenthesis, "he isn't to be despised for *that*, you know." That's what I said to myself when I learned about Mr. Clarke's brotherhood. I could easily have heard tidings that would have pained me more. But "The Big Trees!" Patience,

friend *Transcript;* you wouldn't, surely, have me bore you any longer now. No, another letter."

16. Pg. 19 King, pp. 33-34 "The first one we approached was the only one of the species in the range of vision, and reared its snuff-colored column among some ordinary firs. How majestic it swelled and towered! My companion and I both exclaimed this is the largest tree we have yet seen; this will measure more than a hundred feet. We gazed a long time at it soaring stem, from which, a hundred feet above us, the branches that shot out bent suddenly upwards, like pictures of the golden candlesticks in the Hebrew temple. It seemed profane to put a measuring tape upon such a piece of organized sublimity. But we wanted to know how much more than a hundred feet could be claimed for it, and I made the trial. It was just fifty-six feet in circuit,--but little more than half the size of the monarchs in Mariposa which it seemed to excel so much in majesty. There were hundred trees in the Mariposa grove larger than this, and all of them together did not make half the impression on me that this one stamped into the brain at the first sight. We need to see the "Mother of the Forest" towering near Trinity Church in New York, and overtopping its spire with a column whose life is older than the doctrine of the Trinity, to appreciate its vastness."

pp. 46-47 "But it is no prosaic water. It is a gush of splendor, a column of concentrated light from heaven. Of course, we turn our horses' heads straight toward it. Soon we dismount, and clamber over the boulders and *debris* around which its disheveled strands are briskly leaping. The rich bass deepens as we rise, and before long we are in a cloud of spray that mounts

and thence again
Returns in an unceasing *shower,* which round
With is unemptied cloud of gentle rain,
Is an eternal April to the ground,
Making it all one emerald."

pp. 54-55   " Like sheet lightning,

Ever brightening,

With a low melodious thunder,

All day and all night it is ever drawn

From the brain of the purple mountain,

Which stands in the distance yonder.

The thunder, however, though certainly melodious, is by no means low, as our readers may imagine, when the measure of the fall s reported to them. At the first leap it clears 1,497 feet; then it tumbles down a series of steep stairways 402 feet, and then makes a jump to the meadows, 518 feet more. The three pitches are in full view, making a fall of more than 2400 feet.

But it is the upper and highest cataract that is most wonderful to the eye, as well as most musical. The cliff is so sheer that there is no break in the body of the water during the whole of its descent of more than a quarter of a mile. It pours in a curve from the summit, fifteen hundred feet, (the height of six Park street spires, remember,) to the basin that hoards it but a moment for the cascades that follow. And what endless complexities and opulence of beauty in the forms and motions of the cataract! It is comparatively narrow at the top of the precipice, although as we said, the tide that pours over is thirty-five feet broad. But it widens as it descends, and curves a little on one side as it widens, so that it shapes itself, before it reaches its first bowl of granite, into the figure of the comet that glowed on our sky two years ago. More beautiful than the comet, however, we can see the substance of this water loveliness ever renew itself, and ever pour itself away. Our readers have seen the splendid rockets, on Fourth of July nights, that burst into the serpents of fire. This cataract seems to shoot out a thousand serpentine heads or knots of water, which wriggle down deliberately through the air, and expend themselves in mist before half the descent is over. Then a new set burst from the body and sides of the fall, with the same fortune on the remaining distance; and thus the most charming fretwork of watery nodules, each trailing its vapory train for a hundred feet, or more, is woven all over the cascade, which swings, now and then, thirty feet each way on the mountain side, as if it were a pendulum of watery lace. Once in a while, too, the wind manages to get back of the fall, between it and the cliff, and then it will whirl it round and round for two or three hundred feet, as if it were determined to try to experiment of twisting it to wring it dry. We could lie for hours before Mr. Peck's door, never tired in gazing on this cataract, but ever hungry for more of the witcheries of motion and grace that refine and soften its grandeur."

pp. 64-65

"The flashing mass foams shaking the abyss,

As if to sweep down all things in its track,

Charming the eye with dread---a matchless cataract!

Just about the time we made our visit, Mr. [Nathaniel Parker] Willis was publishing in the *Home Journal* his criticism on the defects of Niagara—not of the cataract, but of its surroundings. Its *lack of mountain,* he says, makes the natural sovereignty of the spot unrecognizable at any distance. "How much more properly Niagara would catch the eye, if quotation-marked with the Hudson Highlands on either side of the Fall, and emphasized with on high mountain peak for a note of admiration!" The great Nevada cataract is arranged on Mr. Willis's principles. The Sierras have put their exclamation point as precisely the right spot. For on the northwest, immediately over it, springs an obelisk of bare granite two thousand feet high, utterly unscaleable on the front, and on its back-line, repeating with surprising exactness the contour of the Matterhorn on its longer side, as drawn in the fourth volume of Ruskin's "Modern Painters," and in Hinchcliff's "Summer Among the Alps." I do not know what splendor of cascade or sublimities of rock the Himalayas hide; but I would venture something on the faith that nowhere on the globe is there a mile of river scenery that will compare with this Sierra glen, through which the Middle Fork of the Merced makes its two glorious plunges under the shadow of granite walls and soaring pinnacles"

Translator's note: For the Biblical citations that were extant in Sozzini's Latin, I simply translated them into English with the rest of the Latin; therefore, they probably will not match exactly with the text in various versions of the Bible; however, the meaning should be the same. I had no way of knowing what language or version of the Bible Fausto was using, (Fausto was proficient in at least seven languages) so I translated Sozzini's printed Latin to English.

In the cases that I have added Biblical text to the Sozzini's prose for better understanding, I have footnoted those texts. All added Biblical text has come from the New American Bible, Saint Joseph edition.

Glossary

Arian-Arians: adj. An Arian is a believer in a theology that stems from Arius, a fourth century theologian. This adjective historically has been used very loosely to accuse people who hold any theological position that does not put Jesus equal in power or eternal nature with God. Sozzini objects strongly to being called an Arian, and explains very clearly his difference in religious opinion with the theology of Arius. As an aside, there is no historical connection between Adolph Hitler's "Aryan Race" and this adjective.

Ascension-Primary Ascension: n. The ascent of Jesus into Heaven after his death on the cross. Sozzini, in his theology, differs with traditional Christianity by claiming that there were more than one ascension by Jesus Christ.

Atonement: n. One of the best definitions that I have ever heard of this word was by a Unitarian Pastor; he broke the word down into its parts "at-one-ment". He then went on to explain how all human experience should be viewed as connected as a whole, and we should attempt to understand and learn from our "human at-one-ment." The traditional Christian understanding of atonement is the uniting of humans to God through the love and sacrifice of Jesus Christ. Here again, Sozzini differs in his theological opinion with traditional Christianity. You could say, Sozzini arrives at the same place, i.e., humans united with God, but uses a different route to get there.

Creation, Creature, New Creature n. The word creature admits to a creation (or making of life by God). In theology there are multiple concepts connected with these nouns. Sozzini attempts to clear up confusion over these concepts. He sees the original making of the world as very separate from the creation of the kingdom of Jesus Christ.

Apostles' Creed from the Book of Common Prayer 1662 AD:

I believe in God the Father Almighty,

Maker of heaven and earth,

And in Jesus Christ, his only Son, our Lord,

Who was conceived by the Holy Ghost,

Born of the Virgin Mary,

Suffered under Pontius Pilate,

Was crucified, died, and was buried;

He descended into hell;

On the third day he rose again from the dead;

He ascended into heaven

And sitteth on the right hand of God the Father Almighty;

From thence he shall come to judge the quick and the dead.

I believe in the Holy Ghost;

The holy Catholic Church;

The Communion of Saints;

The Forgiveness of sins;

The Resurrection of the body,

And Life everlasting.

Amen.

Nicene Creed from first council of Nicea 325 AD:

We believe in one God, the Father Almighty, Maker of all things visible and invisible

And in one Lord Jesus Christ, the Son of God, begotten of the Father (the only-begotten; that is, of the essence of the Father, God of God), Light of Light, Very God of Very God, begotten, not made, being of one substance with the Father,

By whom all things were made (both in heaven and on earth);

Who for us men, and for our salvation, came down and was incarnate and was made man;

He suffered, and the third day he rose again, ascended into heaven;

From thence he shall come to judge the quick and the dead.

And in the Holy Ghost.

(But those who say: 'There was a time when he was not;' and 'He was not before he was made,' and 'He was made out of nothing,' or 'He is of another substance' or essence,' or 'The Son of God is created, 'or changeable,' or 'alterable'---they are condemned by the holy catholic and apostolic Church.)

Death: n. In almost all theology (Christian included) death only affects the body; i.e., the body dies, while the spirit lives on. Sozzini sees a more complete death, and this makes his opinions at once interesting and challenging. He sees salvation as eternal life and the wages of sin as horrible death.

Divine: adj. and Divinity; n. (Holy, Sacred of God) Socinians have been accused historically for denying the divinity of Jesus Christ, i.e., Jesus not being equal to God in all ways. There is some truth to this, but like all propaganda, it is only partly true. Sozzini explains the divinity of Jesus as being bestowed by God after the resurrection. Further, like much of Socinianism when compared with traditional Christian teaching, Sozzini arrives at a very similar result on this issue; i.e., Jesus is eternal and one in purpose and power with God in the end.

God's Nature: n. Gods Nature is considered in most Christian theology to be a separate profound mystery that lies at the core of all creation.

Gospel: n. the teachings of Jesus Christ

Intercession: n. In traditional Christian theology, Jesus has made an intercession on our behalf in order to bring us back to God.

Intermediary: n. In traditional Christian theology Jesus is between God and Man as savior and advocate.

Human Nature: n. All of that which is only contained in being human

Justification: n. In theology this represents a balancing of the scales of justice between God and man. Sozzini argues that an act of justification, in a sense, is not necessary, because God does not require it.

Placation: n. a payment in full; in traditional Christian theology this implies a satisfaction or repayment for human sin.

Polemicist: n. One that advances an argument through the use of a polemic. From the Greek *polemikos or polemos, in reference to war, i.e., two conflicting views or opinions.*

Propitiation: n. from the transitive verb, propitiate; In traditional Christian theology, an act that brings about goodwill between God and Man.

Priesthood: n. In traditional Christian theology, it is a conferred power and duty to further the goals of the Gospel of Jesus Christ. In Socinianism, this is centered in the idea of Jesus forgiving our sins, i.e., in part, it lacks a class of priests.

Redemption: n. In traditional Christian theology, Jesus is the "Redeemer" who through his act of atonement (bearing the sins of the world) and sacrifice on the cross, saves us from sin. Again Sozzini has a very different view of this. He sees the sacrifice on the cross as the result of the challenge of Jesus Christ to the polity of his time, and an ultimate act of obedience to God, and it is the message of Jesus, and his obedience to God, that is the most important to understand, and emulate.

Remission of Sins: n. In traditional Christian theology, Jesus won a victory for the remission of our sins by his act of atonement and sacrifice, i.e., we are not saved by our works, but by the grace of Jesus Christ. Sozzini explains a different kind of remission, i.e., a remission granted from God by obedience to the teaching of Jesus Christ. Thus, the early Unitarians insisted on practicing the nonviolence preached by Jesus Christ in the Sermon on the Mount.

Salvation: n. In traditional Christian theology this word represents a return of humans to God having been freed from sin. With Sozzini, this concept carries more weight in life as a thing of itself.

Spirit: n. the non-material force or essence behind life

Time: n. time for us humans is sequential; in most theology time is eternal

Trinity, Holy: n. God the Father, His son Jesus Christ, and the Holy Ghost comprise the Christian Trinity. In traditional Christianity, they are believed to be co-eternal and co-substantial "true God from true God."

Word: n. "Word" in theology is akin to "World;" i.e., the meanings can be very plastic. The "Word" can mean Jesus, the Gospel, and incarnation, a message, and other things, like in the case with the word "World," one needs to look closely at context. As an aside here, the words "World" and "Word" in theology have led to a great deal of dispute among theologians.

World: n. The word "World" in theology can mean planet Earth, spirit world, world to come, heavenly world, transitional world, sinful world, and I have undoubtedly left out some other possibilities. When this word is used theologically, one really has to look for the context.

BIBLIOGRAPHY

Allen, Joseph Henry. <u>A Historical Sketch of the Unitarian Movement Since the Reformation</u>, New York, The Christian Literature Co. 1894 reprint by Bibliolife

Cantu, Cesare. "Discorso XXXVIII "Antitrinitari, I Soccini II <u>Biandrata" Gle Eretici D'Italiaa Discorsi Storici,</u> Vol II. Torino, 1866.

Chalmers, F.S.A. <u>The General Biographical Dictionary</u>, London 1816. Reprint A M S Press, Inc., New York 1969

Cory, David Monroe. <u>Faustus Socinus</u>, Boston 1932.

Emerson, Ralph Waldo. <u>Nature</u> from <u>Nature Walking</u>, by Ralph Waldo Emerson and Henry David Thoreau. Beacon Press, Boston, Mass 1991 original publication 1836

Encyclopedia Britannica. CD Version. 1999. "Emerson, Ralph Waldo"

Florida, R. E. <u>Studies on Voltaire and the Eighteenth Century.</u> Vol. 122 "Voltaire and the Socinians," Oxford 1974

Johnston, Hank. <u>The Yosemite Grant 1864-1906 A Pictorial History</u>. The Yosemite Association 2008

King James Version. The Holy Bible. 1611 American Bible Society, New York

King, Thomas Starr. A Vacation among the Sierras Yosemite in 1860. The Book Club of California 1962. (Taken from a series of articles that appeared in the Boston Evening Transcript in late 1860 and early 1861)

Kot, Stanislas, trans. From the Polish by Wilbur, Earl Morse. Socinianism in Poland. Boston 1957

Rees, Thomas F.S.A. "Historical Introduction", The Rocavian Catechism. London, 1818. Reprinted Lexington, Kentucky 1962 reprint by General Books

Rev. Riches De Levante, Edward, A.M. PHD. The Hexaglot Bible Comprising the Holy Scriptures of the Old and New Testaments in the Original Tongues. New York. Funk and Wagnalls Co. 1906

Shirley, Sargent. Galen Clark. Flying Spur Press, Third Edition. 1994

Smith, G. Abbot, D.D., D.C.L., LL. D., A Manual Greek Lexicon of the New Testament. First Edition 1921. Reprinted 1960

Sozzino, Fausto. Operia Omnia. Vol. I. Irenopoli, 1656. pp. 650-676

The New American Bible Saint Joseph Edition. Catholic Book Publishing Co. 1991

Webster's Dictionary. New World Dictionary of the American Language Second College Edition. New York. 1978

Wolfe, Linnie Marsh. Son of the Wilderness. 1947. Alfred A Knopf, New York

.

115

Made in the USA
Columbia, SC
22 September 2018